SCHOOLS FOR OUR TIME

The Local Classroom in an Uncertain World

Allen E. Salowe

A SCARECROWEDUCATION BOOK

The Scarecrow Press, Inc.
Lanham, Maryland, and Oxford
2003

A SCARECROWEDUCATION BOOK

Published in the United States of America
by Scarecrow Press, Inc.
A Member of the Rowman & Littlefield Publishing Group
4501 Forbes Boulevard, Suite 200, Lanham, MD 20706
www.scarecrowpress.com

PO Box 317
Oxford
OX2 9RU, UK

British Library Cataloguing in Publication Information Available

Library of Congress Cataloging-in-Publication Data

Salowe, Allen E.
    Schools for our time : the local classroom in an uncertain world /
Allen E. Salowe.
        p. cm.
    "A ScarecrowEducation book."
    Includes bibliographical references and index.
    ISBN 0-8108-4709-4 (pbk. : alk. paper)
    1. Community and school—United States. 2. Educational
sociology—United States. I. Title.
LC221 .S25 2003
371.19'0973—dc21

                                                        2002154846

⊗™ The paper used in this publication meets the minimum requirements of
American National Standard for Information Sciences—Permanence of Paper
for Printed Library Materials, ANSI/NISO Z39.48-1992.
Manufactured in the United States of America.

OTHER BOOKS BY ALLEN SALOWE

Prostate Cancer: Overcoming Denial with Action, A Guide to Screening, Treatment, and Healing (St. Louis, Mo.: Quality Medical Publishing, 1997; New York: St. Martins Press, 1998).

With Leon M. Lessinger:
Game Time: The Educator's Playbook for the New Global Economy (Lancaster, Penn.: Technomic Press, 1997).
Healing Public Schools: The Winning Prescription to Cure Their Chronic Illness (Lanham, Md.: Scarecrow Press, 2001).
Solutions: Tools and Strategies for Schools (Lanham, Md.: Scarecrow Press, 2002).
The Solutions Fieldbook: Tools and Strategies for Schools (Lanham, Md.: Scarecrow Press, 2002).

With William Kiefer:
Shape Up Your Local School: A 100-Page Primer for Improving Public Education (Lanham, Md.: Scarecrow Press, 2002).

CONTENTS

Foreword   ix

Introduction   1

1 The Continuous Loop   5
   Connections to the Larger Community   6
   Leaving Students Behind   8
   Bridging the Opportunity Gap   8
   A Disgraceful Report   9
   The Local School   11
   An Even Larger Problem   12
   Schools Meet the Needs of Their Time   13
   A Qualitatively Different Local School for Our Time   17
   The Needs of Our Times   18

2 Readying Culturally Diverse Students for Their Time   23
   Where We Have Come From   24
   Where Does This Leave the Local School?   29
   A Crisis of Higher U.S. Dropout Rates   30

3 New Standards of Competitiveness   37
   Economic Perspective   37

Free-Market Global Economy   39
Adam Smith's View of Economic Growth   40
The Global Mind-set   50
Customer-Focused Quality   51
Suddenly, a New Beginning   52

4 The Local School Needs Direction   55
Searching for Direction   55
The Gap between the Building and Classroom Performance   59
Why Children Can't Walk to School   60
Turning Our Backs on the Problem   62
Community Planning and School Planning   64
Coordinating School Facilities and Community Planning   66

5 Initiatives for Local School Improvement   71
Local and State Initiatives   71
Teacher Backlash to Cut the Links   76
The Missing Links in the Local School   78
Initiatives Linking Industries and Learning   79
Linking Parents to the Local School   82

6 Partnering: Smoothing the Transition   85
Linking Classroom to Career   86
Putting Classroom-to-Career Programs into Practice   87
Students Show the Way   88
A New Approach to Learning   89
The Employer's Role   91
Classroom-to-Career Case Studies   96

7 Classroom-to-Career Programs: Best Practices   105
Success Stories Show the Way   105
The Building Blocks of Classroom-to-Career Initiatives   111
The Local School Starts Good Practices Early   116
What Schools Need from Business Partners   117
From High Tech to High Touch   120
Turning the Tide   122
The Vision of Success   123
Using Measures That Work   124
Using Refrigerator-Door Language   125

8 Focusing on Our Time 127
The Unavoidable Link of Our Time 127
Easier Said Than Done 128
Idleness Breeds Trouble 129
Three Ds and the Three Rs 130
Teachers Set the Tone 131
A Single Set of Rules 132
The Apple Doesn't Fall Far from the Tree 134
Teachers Need Classes in Classroom Management
and Control 136
Teachers Are Not Automatically Skilled in Urban Stress 137
The Career Academy 139

9 Leveraging What We Know 145
We Cannot Understand a System until We Try to Change It 147
First, We Need Focus 148
Where We Start 152
Examine the Puzzle Carefully 154
Why Are We Here? 154
The Deming Effect 155
Outer-Ring Pieces Link with Classroom-to-Career Initiatives 161
The Middle Ring and Classroom-to-Career Initiatives 164
The Rubber Hits the Road in the Inner Circle 165
At the Center: The Classroom 165

10 Classroom-to-Career Programs and the Future 167
Classroom-to-Career Time Horizon: Twenty Years 168
The Teacher's Job: Make the Work Challenging 170
Implications 177
Leadership and Vision 180
The Global Economy 184

11 The Diverse Workforce 187
The New Melting Pot 188
Managing Knowledge Means Managing Oneself 190
Abundance of Choices 191
High-Performing Schools Align Action and Values 193
Leading Transition: A New Model for Change 195

Taking the Long View   197
Schools Cannot Be All Things to All People and Succeed   200

Index   203

About the Author   207

FOREWORD

People belong to their time and the schools belong to the people.

—Adapted from a Hebrew proverb

Throughout history, schools have existed for a special purpose—to serve the common good in a way that meets the changing needs of the time. Allen Salowe's past works have concentrated on providing reliable tools and strategies for improving schools, illustrating that the know-how exists. In this work, Salowe invites the reader to explore what is so different about our time in history, what response is required of the people's schools, and why that response is so slow in coming even when we know what works. He openly and candidly wonders whether we must first learn more about ourselves as people—our strengths, our values, our place in the world—in order to understand what we need from our schools so that we might exercise that understanding. Looking beyond the ingredients for good schools, he outlines the conditions in which good schools can thrive and invites us to ask ourselves, as educators and community leaders, such challenging questions as:

- What is so different about this time in our country's history?
- What if a qualitatively different local school is required to meet the people's needs in this unique time? But what if the people have yet

to learn who they are and, therefore, can see the problem, voice the problem, but do very little as a culture to actively solve the problem?

- What priority would get placed on our schools and their improvement if the community collectively understood the continuous loop between quality education opportunities and social and economic success?
- What if there are built-in features that absolutely bar schools' ability (not their willingness) to leave no child behind?
- What should the people do?

I live and work in a community struggling to answer these questions—a diverse community in which both the schools and the economic and social stability have been in serious decline. Four years ago, community leaders took on the difficult task of revitalizing our community. The improvement of our schools is a central tenet in these revitalization efforts. We have concentrated on two broad themes: *building capacity* inside the school system to significantly improve teaching and learning and to sustain those improvements over time, and *building public will* so that the community demands and takes the actions necessary to ensure good schools.

As Salowe contends, doing the former is a formidable but doable task. It requires an unrelenting focus on students and data, intensive ongoing professional development of staff, personalized learning opportunities and choice, targeted resources and support, and a range of partners and allies. In essence, it requires a willingness to invest in and implement well what we know works, including making tough decisions about the abandonment of past practices that belong in exactly that—the past!

Connecting schools to the larger community (i.e., ensuring that schools meet the needs of the time) is an equally important task of school and community leaders, but, as Salowe notes, here is where common good and political realities often collide. Here also is where we come full circle as a country in how we balance the common good and the special purpose of the local school. Is the school's task to well educate an increasingly diverse population (e.g., to ensure that all students achieve the reading, writing, listening, speaking, and mathematical skills they need to be successful employees, employers, and citizens) or is it to continue to be the agent of social reform and social integration? As Salowe asks, "Can schools really be all things to all people and succeed?"

In Lancaster, as in many urban areas, the task of educating all children is made significantly more difficult by high levels of poverty, language barriers, homelessness, and an increasing array of students with special academic and social needs. In Lancaster, as in many places, common good, special purpose, and political realities continually collide. Two things have helped us to create and maintain a steady course, to grapple openly with these issues, and to make progress despite the challenges. One is a living, strategic plan that reflects a commitment to things we deeply care about—the success of our students, the quality of our practice, and our connections with families and the community. Six main ideas form the basis for this set of strategies designed to help us build both capacity and public will:

1. An audacious plan, goal, and vital signs that act as signposts and help to mobilize all stakeholders.
2. Coherent core beliefs that guide our journey.
3. Trust in ourselves, each other, and in the goals and strategies as the foundation for accomplishment.
4. Excellence in teaching and learning to accelerate student success.
5. Empowering relationships with stakeholders to enroll the whole community.
6. Essential supports to facilitate sustained student success and staff performance at all levels.

The second element that has kept our work and progress steady is the implementation of ISO 9001. ISO 9001 is a business-oriented, quality system that is being increasingly employed in service organizations, including school districts. The basic mantra of the ISO system is to "say what you do, do what you say, and prove it." Adopting the ISO standards has brought greater discipline to our work in Lancaster, ensuring that we are using data effectively, implementing each new strategy consistently, maintaining institutional knowledge, attending to customer satisfaction, increasing efficiency, preventing or rapidly responding to problems, and creating a culture of continuous improvement. ISO does not ensure that we have chosen the right educational strategies but, rather, it brings a high degree of discipline to the *implementation* so that we know when a strategy is or is not working and can respond appropriately.

Our quality system (ISO 9001) is a core part of the reason why Lancaster is becoming an entire system of good schools rather than a few isolated examples. It takes all the stakeholders in the system to implement ISO and cycles of deeper implementation (i.e., getting better with every annual audit) are required to maintain ISO registration. Although it requires an enormous amount of work early on, ISO is much less painful to implement and is much more easily bought into and owned by the entire system than initial perception might indicate, and the long-term dividends far exceed the investment.

Both the strategic plan and the implementation of ISO have been crucial to our efforts to build systemwide capacity internally in the district as well as to increase the community's desire (i.e., public will) to support and to help us sustain our work. Internal and external stakeholders can articulate our strategic plan, goals, and targets and they view ISO as a strong indicator that we are using our resources (human and capital) wisely.

While we still have many challenges ahead and are by no means at the level of progress to which we aspire, the pace of our improvement is startling. Perhaps that is most attributable to our willingness in Lancaster to confront the questions Salowe is raising, even though we know there are no simple solutions—just deep soul searching about what we most need and care about and the willingness to shoulder the hard work it takes to make it happen. In doing so, we stand as part of—and not apart from—our community.

It is this kind of tough questioning that Salowe commends us, as educators and community leaders, to do. This is not necessarily the only time in our history in which the level of connectedness and integration Salowe describes between schools and community is necessary, but it may be the first time in which we have faced such difficulty in determining both the special purpose and the common good our schools must serve. The content of this book serves as a blunt reminder to keep a stiff spine in the face of those who would see public schools fail. Moreover, it reminds those of us who would see public schools succeed that we must be willing to shoulder both the accountability for the performance of our schools *and* our share of responsibility for the community as a whole.

In Salowe's words, we (educational leaders) must contribute to the "score" (music). Otherwise there is only noise.

—Vicki Phillips, Superintendent
First ISO 9001 Registered School District in North America
Lancaster, Pennsylvania

INTRODUCTION

It's been more than thirty years since a well-aimed bullet felled Dr. Martin Luther King Jr. My peaceful hometown erupted that day; a mob kicked and stomped a policeman to death. The New Jersey National Guard, complete with their tanks and guns, was brought in to calm the fury.

For many years, Plainfield, New Jersey, had been a prosperous suburban commuter town with neat tree-lined streets, sending bankers and professionals off to New York City on the commuter train. The city had also been a model of the prosperous Industrial Age with busy factories, ethnically mixed neighborhoods, full employment, and a thriving downtown. Neighborhood schools dotted the landscape and the high school was consider a model academy.

By 1967, times had already started to change. New industrial production processes increased the need for more land to house single-story factory assembly plants. The city's largest employer, Mack Trucks, accepted a better offer and moved its entire factory works and its jobs to Maryland. The better-paid workers left also.

The old four-story Mack plant was gradually converted to smaller shops with fewer jobs that paid less. The unemployment level steadily crept higher. The once-clean streets lined with neat rows of houses owned by the industrial workers gave way to a shrinking tax base that caused these houses to be subdivided into more affordable apartment units to house two or more families each. Less costly housing attracted a sharp change in the mix of persons looking to live in less and less costly shelters and looking for fewer and fewer jobs. These underemployed residents could only afford marginal rents in what became rapidly became seriously neglected housing and neighborhoods.

Almost overnight, the public schools lost more than 20 percent of their student population to private and parochial schools. Parents who could afford to escape deteriorating school performance paid for the opportunity to change with their own money. There was no thought of such options as vouchers to help parents and students run away from declining school performance. School buses carted the remaining public school students twice daily across the small, three-square-mile city. The mix of 10,000 public school students shifted almost overnight to 93 percent minority. For all intents and purposes, the school system had become more severely segregated but the court order to bus children to desegregate neighborhood schools quickly became obsolete though remaining in force for another twenty-five years.

The city council and school board stopped speaking to one another for more than five years. It took the intervention of the famed Menninger Clinic of Topeka, Kansas, to come to town and to begin to reverse the deep-seated anger. Stress levels had reached the boiling point in both chambers, spilling over into the living rooms and into the streets. Suddenly, and almost imperceptibly, the bottom had fallen out of the town and its quality of life. In many ways, this small city became a metaphor for the nation's urban ills.

I looked for ways to help relieve the conflicts and to help promote healing, offering to do anything, even sweep the streets on my weekends. The mayor asked me to take a spot on the city planning board and later appointed me to the school board, where I eventually was chosen its president. The unexpected events and initiatives that followed led to my changing my professional career to urban and community planning and to a lifelong interest in improving public education.

All along, but wrongly, I'd assumed Plainfield had been the exception during those stressful times and that there was some natural link between the local school board and the local general-purpose government—but, in fact, I was to learn that such disconnections were there between the employment sector and the city's schools as well.

To this day, local school boards and their local general-purpose government—whether it be a county commission, a city commission, or town council—lack a partnership focus and commitment when it comes to the local public schools. Each is left to go its own way as though the action of one part of the body had no bearing upon another part.

In *Head to Head*, MIT professor Lester Thurow sums it up clearly: "Local governments don't want to pay for first-class schools. They know that less than half the population has children in school at any one time, that students will leave home and use their skills in different geographic regions of the country, and that high taxes necessary to pay for good schools would drive industry away. Firms would locate next door and free ride on their well-educated workforce. Someone else should make the necessary investments.[1]

"Communities need to quit using schools as the dumping ground where social problems that cannot be solved elsewhere are assigned. The school's prime responsibility is to ensure that its students are educated. The front lines of the war on crime, drugs, teenage pregnancy, or housing desegregation need to be established elsewhere. Better nutrition, driver's training, and sports are secondary. The energy of our school systems should be focused on education—not dissipated on other goals, no matter how laudable."[2]

Whether we admit it or not, we are now immersed in a free-market, information-driven global economy that is full of great uncertainties. It calls for greater interaction between the schools and their local "partners." Schools cannot do it all alone. They need cooperation to adapt outdated classroom methods to today's student thinking and behavior in a new world already upon us. Likewise, a local government cannot go it alone. It cannot guide a community in its more challenging economic role in what is a ferociously competitive economy without the backing of an effective school system. This is what the classroom-to-career initiatives are all about. What happens in today's classroom bears directly on tomorrow's student career.

At the end of the day, there is need for more, not less, interdependent action between the school and the local community to:

- Connect the classroom with employer needs.
- Help students meet twenty-first-century workplace demands.

- Guide local educators to meeting new local needs.
- Rebuild neighborhood pride in their local schools.
- Foster stakeholder involvement in the local schools.
- Define citizenship standards to be met by students.
- Prepare students for knowledge work.
- Equalize classroom-teaching quality across every local school.
- Understand the meaning of information moving at the speed of light.
- Promote businesslike practices in local school management.
- Link mistakes made with lessons learned.

In America, the quality of life is nourished by a good job, so the forging of a strong working relationship between the classroom and the real world—from classroom to career—is more than academic. It needs to bring together what's needed for students, teachers, and stakeholders. It gives kids a reason for showing up each day in class. It gives teachers a focus for problem-based learning. It links the classroom with the real world.

More than a century ago, John Dewey urged educators: "Relate the school to life, and all studies are of necessity correlated."[3]

We say today, what is started by passion is pursued by conviction.

NOTES

1. Lester Thurow, *Head to Head: The Coming Economic Battle among Japan, Europe, and America* (New York: Morrow, 1992), 274.

2. Thurow, *Head to Head*, 279.

3. John Dewey, *The School and Society* (Chicago: University of Chicago Press, 1900).

1

THE CONTINUOUS LOOP

Ninety percent of teens say school would be more interesting and meaningful if it were taught in connection with careers.[1]

—*Teen Attitudes toward Work*, 1994

Local school quality is a two-way street—a continuous loop of cause and effect.

First, local school quality directly determines the attractiveness of the community to new residents, to new businesses, and to new jobs. Local school performance helps create quality neighborhoods, bring new jobs, stimulate a vibrant economy, and build a strong tax base to underpin the community's financial structure. The community's quality of life, in part, flows from the quality of the local school.

Second, stagnant school performance "browns the grass" on this side of the street for local residents, existing businesses, and knowledge workers. Each depends on the local school for different reasons. When the local school falls down on the job of delivering skills-ready students ready for work, then local residents, businesses, and industry start looking for "greener" grass.

In the 1980s, Florida led the nation in planning by spearheading compulsory comprehensive land use and infrastructure planning for all local governments. Yet more than twenty years passed before Florida equated the importance of the local schools to its local economic environment and made mandatory the inclusion of school facilities planning in local "comprehensive" plans.

This is not unusual. The local school failed to see its connection to the larger community. Worse yet, school policies cut off the larger community from the local school.

CONNECTIONS TO THE LARGER COMMUNITY

In 2001, *Imaging the Region,* a report published by the Florida Atlantic University/Florida International University Joint Center for Urban and Environmental Problems, quoted the South Florida Regional Planning Council on the link between the poor-performing local school and the region's future. Paraphrasing the report:

1. Generally speaking, poor-performing schools adversely impact future performance of students who attend them, as well as a range of private investment decisions by existing residents and investment interests.
2. On the human side, lower-performing schools tend to be attended predominantly by poorer, minority students who have limited school-selection choices. Lower levels of educational attainment are related to lower levels of achievement in the later stages of life and result in a continuing cycle of poverty.
3. On a regional scale, reinvestment in lower-performing schools and increased school performance promise to be powerful tools for improving the quality of life throughout the region.[2]

Like politics, all schools are local. U.S. House Speaker Tip O'Neill gave us this lesson in his book, *All Politics Is Local.* First and foremost, we need to accept the fact that the local school is there to first serve its local community.

Local school quality affects where people choose to live, where they work, where to invest, the use of roadways, and the quality of neighborhood life. No matter how often a local school board redistricts and how many big yellow school buses it decides to operate, "Bad schools are a reason for leaving a part of a region or abandoning a region altogether."[3]

- Other study findings have broad application across the nation.
- Schools and public safety affect where people choose to live; this significantly contributes to the impact on road construction and usage.
- In order of preference, good schools, privacy, and a neighborhood with a sense of community rank first through third among 600 study respondents.
- Living near the office or job as a quality-of-life indicator ranked lowest; people will trade off commuting for better schools and communities.
- Quality-of-life study respondents rank their own local schools lowest.
- Whites rate their public schools lower than do Hispanics and blacks. Blacks rate government and police lower than do Hispanics and whites. Suburbanites were more satisfied with the job done by their local school and government than were their city-dwelling counterparts.
- Across the region, crime and public school quality rank highest on the list of concerns. Crime was highest for Miami-Dade County residents. Quality of schools was highest for Palm Beach County residents. Too many unsupervised children and teenagers was the highest concern in Broward County.
- Public school quality concerns were almost twice as high for this region than for the national sample. The public views low public school quality as a "most important problem" and consistent with the poor job rating given to schools.

A region can build its human capital in two ways: by attracting those persons already skilled and by educating its own residents, especially the young. The kind of school needed to grow the human capital of residents is an important attractor for educated employees or businesses considering relocating to South Florida and across the nation. And bad schools are a valid reason for leaving a part of a region or abandoning the region altogether.

LEAVING STUDENTS BEHIND

A strong measure of how good a job the local school, region, or nation is doing in preparing a competent workforce for the new free-market global economy is found in how well its high school graduates score on college entrance exams that qualify them for admission to top competitive schools.

The 1.3 million Scholastic Aptitude Test (SAT) takers entering college in the fall 2001 included the largest number of minority students in history, comprising more than a third of all test takers.

Even though SAT scores have risen minimally over the past ten years, just under 80 percent of test takers scored less than 1200. The average SAT score for admission to Florida State University, by contrast, is 1238; at Washington State University, 1243; and at Kansas State University, 1450.[4] Only 587 students (.0005 percent!) scored a perfect 1600. When 80 percent of our students score less than the average for state universities across the country, we are misleading the students who need us the most.

One encouraging sign is that students reported higher academic aspirations than students of the past. More than half of all 2001 college-bound students planned to pursue master's or doctoral degrees.

BRIDGING THE OPPORTUNITY GAP

Seeing the SAT scores increase, even if only gradually, and seeing our students aim higher is encouraging—but there are other troubling realities needing consideration. Nationally, scores for many ethnic and minority groups continue to lag behind and a gender gap, though narrowed, still persists.

Gaps for different racial, ethnic, and socioeconomic groups seen on the SAT also appear on virtually every measure of achievement, including other standardized tests and classroom grades. These reveal themselves as early as fourth grade. Such differences illustrate a persistent social problem in our country: inequitable access to high-quality education.

Data on 2001 SAT test takers offers a glimmer of hope that the opportunity gap can be narrowed through greater access to rigorous coursework, but researchers find that such access varies greatly across racial and ethnic groups. For instance:

- Forty-nine percent of white students studied high school physics; only forty percent of African American students did so.
- Fifty-nine percent of Asian American students report taking pre-calculus; just thirty-four percent of Puerto Ricans report taking this course.[5]

Once again, it points up the need for urgent steps to increase the access and exposure of minority and low-income students to higher quality K–12 education. It also means radically improving curricula, teacher training, and accountability in all schools—elementary through twelfth grade. This really means "equalizing" classroom teaching performance across K–12. A racially imbalanced school district (because its student population is primarily minority) whose schools perform on an unequal basis (because its school classrooms do not perform on a consistent basis) is as unacceptable as the "separate but equal" schools of the old South.

A DISGRACEFUL REPORT

The first annual report to Congress on teacher quality nationwide, *Meeting the Highly Qualified Teachers Challenge*, showed that state certification systems allow too many teachers lacking solid subject-content knowledge into the classroom.

The sixty-six-page report by the U.S. Department of Education said a handful of states, including New York, Texas, and North Carolina, had begun raising requirements for qualifying teachers but it also strongly criticized the majority of states for lax standards. As an example, it noted that a mandatory test required of all California teachers, the California Basic Educational Skills Test, is set at the tenth-grade level.[6]

States also set passing grades on another common test that assesses a teacher's reading, writing, and math skills "shockingly low," the report to Congress said. Of twenty-nine states using the qualifying exam, known as the Praxis Pre-Professional Skills Test, only Virginia ranks passing at a score at roughly the national average in reading. Fifteen states pass teachers who read in the lowest quarter of the national average, and nine states pass teachers in the bottom fifth of all readers.

In a speech to teacher-training specialists, Education Secretary Rod Paige noted that ill-prepared teachers were heavily concentrated among poor children. About 43 percent of math teachers in poor neighborhoods, for example, lacked a background in math, compared with 27 percent in wealthier neighborhoods.

"We're talking about helping children so far down on the achievement scale they're not even a blip on the radar," Paige said. He noted that on national reading tests, "Forty percent of white fourth graders can read while only 12 percent of black fourth graders can read [with facility]."

Congress ordered annual reports starting in 2002 amid concerns about teacher quality. The law requires states to put "highly qualified" teachers in every high-poverty classroom by September 2002 and in all schools by 2005.

"We now have concrete evidence that smart teachers with solid content knowledge have the greatest effect on student achievement," Paige said. "If we are to meet the challenge of having a highly qualified teacher in every classroom by the 2005–06 school year, states and universities must take heed and act now to bring more of these people into our nation's classrooms. There is much to be done, but we know what it is and have no time to waste if no child is to be left behind."[7]

The report said that forty-three states indicate that more than 90 percent of their teachers had full credentials, and that four of them contended that no teachers relied on state waivers of certification requirements. Beyond the skepticism in the report itself, Education Trust, a Washington-based group that represents schools in low-income neighborhoods, said the assertions by the states were at odds with national data and other information. Some school districts concede that up to 25 percent of the district's teachers use provisional licenses that incorporate a deadline for becoming fully qualified teachers.

But a true national commitment to broadly increase student achievement and opportunity is far from being a fact of life. The commitment begins when we can successfully link local community needs with the local school.

It's hard to imagine a groundswell of school–community teamwork without making it a reality at the local community level. And we can only achieve higher levels of social and economic success when we honestly face head on our greatest national security threat: the inequity of access to quality educational opportunity.

THE LOCAL SCHOOL

Brown vs. Board of Education set right a great wrong by overturning segregated schools, but it left local school districts with widespread problems and some unintended consequences.

First, *Brown* permanently unraveled the neighborhood built around the local school, leaving cities and towns with continuous uncertainty. By so doing, it sapped the strength and connection between the local school and its natural constituency.

Second, and more importantly, it exposed the fissure in the "equalizing" effort. The focus on quality classroom teaching performance was shifted to maximizing social goals.

As a result, a generation or more of schoolchildren since *Brown* has been shifted around to artificially racially balance schools while selling short the need for broad-based quality education. And with it, scores of educators have left the profession in frustration.

Uncertainties have flowed through the minds of parents, local residents, businesspersons, and employers annually. How would each plan for its own future?

The value of housing in large part determines the mix of residents—wealthy, middle-income, and low-income—living in different neighborhoods, but we need to keep in mind that housing is fixed, nailed and cemented to the ground. Only people are movable. Where we choose to make our home directly impacts the social and economic mix of school populations and jurisdictions.

Further compounding the unintended consequences of disconnecting the local school from its environs, some 440,000 yellow school buses now cart children from here to there and back again, creating a spatial planning dilemma. Road capacities are heavily strained at peak school transportation times. Children are separated from neighbors and friends and thrown into school situations that prove to be unnecessarily stressful and nonproductive. The school bus schedule becomes the tail that wags the dog.

As an example, for the 2002–2003 school year, the Lee County School Board (Ft. Myers, Florida, area) set out to save $150,000 a year in transportation costs by having all grade K–6 kids bused to start classes at 7 A.M. and all grade 7–12 start classes at 10:30 A.M. This meant K–6 students catch the bus at about 6:00 A.M. so families need to get moving at about 5 A.M. and getting youngsters off to bed before 9:00 P.M. so that they stand a reasonable chance of catching eight hours of sleep.

Part of the justification for making this change was supported by administrator representations that younger students learn better early in the morning. We find no support except perhaps some anecdotal evidence to justify such assertions. So once again, in order to bring cost efficiency into the bus system, the classroom teacher faces a new dimension of what's happening in the classroom. Still another social complexity is thrust upon mostly ill-prepared teachers.

At this writing, the parents of this district are busily collecting signatures on a petition to reverse this position. The school board is considering yielding on fifteen minutes but in any event, teachers and administrators have a needless distraction as they approach a new school year.

AN EVEN LARGER PROBLEM

The local school must work on these and other nonstudent-centered policies. Certainly there is no shortage of advice and enough critics and detractors to go around, but district policies too often leave the local school and its staff floating out there like a small boat torn away from its mooring.

What happens inside the classroom is what this story is all about. Urban and regional planners lack motivation to connect with issues inside the schoolroom walls. The local general-purpose government turns its eyes away from the economic and social impact of poor-performing schools on the local community. It is inside the classroom where the future economic and social impacts and benefits are being created.

Local planners fixate on equalizing affordable housing opportunities but they have yet to figure out how to define what it takes to keep the grass green on both sides of the street at the same time. It is a continuous loop when:

- Local land-use policies and practices drive local and regional planning; this in turn drives changes in local and regional policies.
- Planners and architects keep trying to create the "city beautiful" by imagining neat town centers, manicured suburbs, pristine rural areas, and environmentally rich and sensitive communities—though affordability eludes them.
- Fads like "new urbanism" take hold, riding the nostalgic dream of workplaces and housing being located close to one another with fewer roads—though reality blocks the way to fulfilling such outdated dreams.

Practically speaking, people must connect with one another no matter what the planner's dream. The yellow school bus carries our children to faraway schools while bringing faraway children to nearby schools. Moms drive their children to school to avoid the disruptive school bus experience. Note the long line of cars on any school day near the entrance starting around 7:20 A.M. and again at 2:20 P.M. In Lee County, the line will soon start at 6:20 A.M. and again at 3:20 P.M.

We use our cars to get to work since our work is seldom located within walking distance of where we live. We drive several miles for groceries because it is economically impractical to maintain a fully stocked 45,000-square-foot supermarket within walking distance of every neighborhood.

Most often, planners concentrate on the "physical" issues while sidestepping the "people" issues. No question, brick and mortar are far easier to plan for than dealing with the unpredictable behavior of people.

Avoiding the impact of regional planning on the local school only serves to further unravel the fabric of the local neighborhood, undermine the local economy, and threaten the quality of school life.

SCHOOLS MEET THE NEEDS OF THEIR TIME

Schools exist to meet the needs of their unique moment in time as well as the need to change with the changing times. To see this more clearly, it helps to step back and examine a chronology of American public schools to see how the patterns of school planning focus on meeting the changing needs of particular moments of time in history.

During colonial times, the Puritans believed it important that everyone be able to read the Bible. Thus began public schooling in America. Under the Old Delauder Satan Act, any town of fifty or more residents was required to pay a man to be the teacher. District schools soon followed in which a town was divided into districts with a school in each of these districts. The view of this period was simple: if you could write enough to sign your name, read the Bible, and decode the meanings of words, then you were educated.

The Northwest Ordinances of 1787 decreed "religion, morality, and knowledge, being necessary to a good government and the happiness of mankind, school and the means for education shall forever be encouraged." It mandated each land township to be divided into thirty-six land sections, with one land section (640 acres) be set aside for public schools. This ordinance still dominates local thinking in many southern and western states.

Free public education was born between 1790 and 1830, but only for poor children; richer people were still expected to pay for their children's schooling. During this period, schools emphasized the discipline and obedient qualities that factory owners of England and America held dear in their workers at the start of the Industrial Revolution.

The numbers of people working in farming dropped between 1830 and 1860 as family farms were gobbled up by larger agricultural businesses. People looked for work in the towns and cities. Cities grew tremendously, fueled by new manufacturing industries, the influx of people from rural areas, and many European immigrants looking for work.

More than 3 million immigrants arrived between 1846 and 1856, a number equal to one-eighth of the entire U.S. population at the time. In these times, the Industrial Revolution needed a docile, obedient, and not-too-educated workforce and looked to the public schools to provide it.

Between 1860 and 1900, Massachusetts passed the first compulsory education law. The goal was making sure that the children of poor immigrants got "civilized" and learned obedience and restraint. Again, the need of the time was creating more good workers who did not contribute to social upheaval.

In *Plessy vs. Ferguson* (1896), the U.S. Supreme Court ruled that Louisiana had the right to require "separate but equal" railroad cars for blacks and whites and thus the federal government officially recognized segregation as legal. Southern states passed strict laws requiring racial segregation in all their public schools, a law not overturned until more than a half-century later. In 1900, only 6.4 percent of seventeen-year-olds finished high school.[8]

By World War I, the size of school boards in the country's twenty-eight biggest cities was cut in half and most local districts or ward-based positions were eliminated in favor of citywide elections. With this action, the local immigrant communities lost control of the local school. Control of the local school board moved from small local businessmen and wage earners to professionals and big businessmen.

The Industrial Age was in full swing between 1900 and 1945 and this helped press changes and demands on schools. The Smith-Hughes Act (1917), pushed by large manufacturers, provided federal funding for vocational education and not by accident did it take job skill training away from trade union apprenticeship programs.

The nation went on to struggle with the Great Depression, and a deadly world war placed new priorities and huge demands on manpower and money. During the Depression, only 16.8 percent of seventeen-year-olds graduated from high school. Just prior to World War II, the graduation rate for this group had reached 50.8 percent.[9] Public education reform took a back seat.

Postwar, New World, and New Demands

American schooling primarily remained the three Rs of "Reading, Writing, and Arithmetic" until the Space Age brought new emphasis on science, math, and engineering. In 1957, Sputnik forced America's schools into more math and science programs to meet this international challenge. The graduation rate of seventeen-year-olds rose to 63.1 percent.[10]

Government-mandated compensatory education programs like Head Start and Title I of the Elementary and Secondary Education Act improved the learning of disadvantaged children. The disadvantaged (physically and culturally disadvantaged) student gained greater recognition.

Brown vs. Board of Education righted the great wrong but it almost tore the nation apart; a half-century later, the schools, especially in the North, were still as segregated as ever.

The 1968–1969 school year witnessed the share of seventeen-year-olds graduating from high school reach an all-time high of 77.1 percent. From that point, the rate has steadily declined—dipping to below 70 percent in 1995–1996.[11]

Milliken vs. Bradley (1974) ruled that schools not be desegregated across school district boundaries. This effectively allowed segregating students of color in inner-city districts from white students in white suburban districts.

Late 1970s to 2003

It's hard to find consensus when it comes to affirmative action in America. Our politicians disagree. Our voters disagree. And now, it appears that even legal arbiters disagree. In 2003, Justice Department lawyers, under orders from President George W. Bush, submitted briefs urging the court of appeals to strike down University of Michigan admissions programs as unconstitutional and arguing that race-neutral alternatives are available to promote diversity.

The California "taxpayers' revolts" led to passage of Proposition 13 and copycat measures like Proposition 2½ in Massachusetts. Such acts froze property taxes, which are still the major source of public school funding. By 1998, California had dropped to forty-third in the nation in per-student spending from having been first just twenty years earlier.

California Proposition 187 (1994) made it illegal for children of undocumented immigrants to attend public school. Though found unconstitutional, anti-immigrant feeling spread across the country and still pervades our thinking in a post–September 11th terrorist-threatened world.

California Proposition 209 (1996) outlawed affirmative action in public employment, public contracting, and public education. A California measure on the June 1998 ballot outlawed bilingual education.

Other states jumped on the bandwagon with their own anti-affirmative action initiatives. In the late 1990s, Florida universities outlawed affirmative action in admissions.

The Free-Market Global Economy Emerges

When we say "small world" now, we really mean it. In a global economy, it's as easy to communicate as it is to order a cup of coffee. International trade and services have surged. More than ever, we live and work in a state of global interconnectedness. In the past, global trade was limited to a narrow, elite, and prosperous slice of the population. Today, the diasporas of India, China, Southeast Asia, and England (to name just a few) are linked by high-speed communications, creating economic challenges to fixed nation-state economies.

Today, a bank moves billions of dollars electronically around to the other side of the globe in milliseconds. A U.S. software company takes orders for a product that was designed in India and manufactured in Ireland to be delivered in France, completely bypassing the United States.

American consumers drive to the shopping mall in an American-branded car but more than likely the vehicle was assembled in Canada. The resurgence of the VW New Beetle was designed in Germany with 25 percent of its parts from the United States, 30 percent of its parts from Canada, and final assembly in Mexico.

At the mall, we look through clothing displays and peek into an electronics store to see a collection of goods made in many different nations. The "made in" labels speak to us, representing a United Nations of producers.

A QUALITATIVELY DIFFERENT LOCAL SCHOOL FOR OUR TIME

Once upon a time, as the old fairy tale goes, an American boy and girl grew up, went to school, raised a family, and were buried all in the same town. Other than dreaming of going to the "big city," Americans never imagined, among other things, that we would one day compete for an economic livelihood against persons schooled thousands of miles away or even on the other side of the globe.

This is free-market competition played out on a global basis and it yields the highest standard of living to the workers of the most successful nation. In this free-market global economy, which is at the same time fraught with less certainty, firms and individuals cooperate when there is a mutual need, sharing risks out of mutual commitment to common objectives. At other times, they are ferocious competitors.

The ongoing advice from U.S. economists is unanimous: In a free-market global economy, American workers can either grow poorer or

learn to compete by thinking and working smarter. American professionals, workers, and managers must compete on the basis of knowledge, effectiveness, quality, and efficiency. This is what we mean by productivity.

To continue delivering the benefits of the American dream, there is
really only one choice for the local school: It needs to better prepare students to go on to improve the quality of their personal performance and
productivity at the same time. If younger and older Americans want the
new free-market jobs, then America's local schools need to do what it
takes to assure the American worker that he or she can keep getting
those higher-paying jobs.

The human capital needed to meet today's free-market competitive
challenge is built on knowledge skills, higher-order thinking skills, and
mind power. This is the primary need of our time and our future.

Knowledge is the primary source of the new economic power. High-
performance organizations are engines that increase productivity, but it
is the quality of human capital, its people, that determines how well the
enterprise can be organized for high performance. Right now, these are
the essential criteria needing to be taught and learned in the local
school. The local school must prepare students to successfully handle a
future built on knowledge.

THE NEEDS OF OUR TIMES

In *A Legacy of Learning* (2000), David T. Kearns and James Harvey argue that a national standard needs to be set so that states and schools are
held accountable.[12] They argue that the American educational system
faces three challenges. First, public schools tend to look at reform but
not do much about it. Second, the education establishment has closed
itself off and is unable to reform. Third, citizens see the problem, voice
the problem, but can do very little as a culture to actively correct it.

The Leave No Child Behind Act signed into law in January 2002 is
the most important piece of federal education legislation since the Elementary and Secondary Education Act of 1965 (ESEA). The central aim
is to tie federal dollars more closely to school and student performance.

The legislation requires local schools to give students annual tests
from the third through eighth grades. These results will be reported to

parents, as well as broken down by race, gender, and other criteria. The act directs money at economically disadvantaged students and struggling schools. The fifty school districts with the highest percentage of such disadvantaged students will immediately get more federal cash.

The money comes with these strings attached:

- Parents of children at schools that continue to fail for several years win the right to transfer their children to better-performing public schools as well as the money to buy after-school education for their children.
- The measure includes a grab bag of other sensible ideas. It gives states a little more flexibility to move money among different federal programs. It sets a timetable for states to make sure that all teachers are qualified to teach their subjects (in terms of traditional school classroom practice, an earth-shattering and long overdue idea).
- It increases spending on reading instruction in the early grades for children with substandard English.

This legislation comes at the apex of the "accountability movement" that has engaged governors' mansions and state legislatures for two decades. But will this bill alone really improve education? We seriously doubt it.

The twin worries of educational reform are overblown expectations and inevitable premature disappointment.

This new legislation totally ignores the chronic problem of achieving systemwide improvement within each local school. To put it more sharply, current and traditional school systems have built-in features that absolutely bar their ability, not their willingness, to "leave no child behind."

In two of the nation's most populous states, the main focus on intergovernmental coordination remains on the physical needs and not the people needs.

- California law requires the school board of the local district to notify the city council or board of supervisors of the city or county within which the school district is located if both of the following findings are supported by clear and convincing evidence: that overcrowding exists in one or more attendance areas within the district, and that all reasonable methods of mitigating the overcrowding have been evaluated and no feasible method for reducing these conditions exists.

• Florida requires that each local plan include clearly stated policies that indicate the future land use categories in which public schools are an allowable use, policies that encourage the location of public schools proximate to urban residential areas, and policies that encourage, to the extent possible, the colocation of other public facilities such as parks, libraries, or community centers with public schools.

From there, the facilities process is concerned with fees, costs, land use, and other development considerations, as well as whole host of nonclassroom-related issues. The school board wants to cite more K–12 "production capacity" and the local government is directed to turn its interest to grabbing "development fees and charges." Neither objective is concerned with school and classroom quality.

A number of years back, James W. Rouse, the visionary developer of Columbia, Maryland, and such urban centers as Boston's Fanuiel Hall and the Baltimore waterfront, told the author, "If you concentrate on what happens between the buildings, the buildings will take care of themselves."

It's what happens inside each school classroom that counts. Schools are the major driver of the Knowledge and Information Age. We read more, talk more, learn and relearn more. Ours is a learning society. Without "learning," the American worker may very well find himself or herself gradually removed from the world of "earning."

NOTES

1. *Teen Attitudes toward Work*, Bruskin Goldring Research, 1994.

2. *Imaging the Region* (Florida Atlantic University/Florida International University Joint Center for Urban and Environmental Problems, 2001), 78.

3. *Imaging the Region*, 73.

4. "Students Review" at www.studentsreview.com/FL/FSU.html (Florida State University); www.studentsreview.com/WA/WSUP.html (Washington State

University); and www.studentsreview.com/KS/KSU.html (Kansas State University); accessed March 3, 2003.

5. "SAT Scores Remain Flat" at CNN.com (August 28, 2001).

6. Diana Jean Schemo, "Education Dept. Says States Have Lax Standards for Teachers" *New York Times* (June 13, 2002).

7. The Secretary's Annual Report on Teacher Quality: Meeting the Highly Qualified Teachers Challenge U.S. Department of Education. (Washington, D.C.: GPO, June 11, 2002).

8. U.S. Department of Education, National Center for Education Statistics, table 101: "High School Graduates Compared with Population 17 Years of Age, by Sex and Control of School: 1839–70 to 1999–2000" (Washington, D.C.: GPO, 2001).

9. U.S. Department of Education.

10. U.S. Department of Education.

11. U.S. Department of Education.

12. David T. Kearns and James Harvey. *Legacy of Learning: Your Stake in Standards and New Kinds of Public Schools* (Washington, D.C.: Brookings Institution Press, 2000).

2

READYING CULTURALLY DIVERSE STUDENTS FOR THEIR TIME

Eighty-five percent of 1,200 registered voters nationwide said they would support "a change in the public schools to place more emphasis on all students preparing for careers and obtaining workforce skills" while in school.[1]

—*Jobs for the Future*, 1997

Suppose for a moment we could, at this time, shrink the Earth's population to a global village of exactly 100 people, with all the existing human ratios remaining the same. What would this compressed global village look like?

According to the Freeman Institute, there would be fifty-seven Asians, twenty-one Europeans, fourteen from the Western Hemisphere (North, South, and Central America), and eight Africans.[2] It also means:

- 70 percent would be nonwhite.
- 70 percent would be non-Christian; only thirty of 100 would be Christian.
- Half of the entire world wealth would be in the hands of only six people; all six persons would be U.S. citizens.
- 70 percent would be unable to read.

- 50 percent would be suffering from malnutrition.
- 80 percent would live in substandard housing.
- Only one would have a college education.

When we consider our world from such an incredibly compressed perspective, it becomes pretty obvious that there is a need for broader understanding and greater mutual respect.

WHERE WE HAVE COME FROM

To better grasp the challenges facing twenty-first-century schools, it is also useful to take a step back to see how we got here. As the twentieth century began to unfold, the stage was set for today's free-market global economy. Previously, we ran through a chronology of U.S. schools. Now we sharpen the focus on how the local school is a creature of its time.

Between the Turn of the Nineteenth Century and Post–World War I (1900–1920)

The United States was a vast and rich country, with most of its territories largely undeveloped and its institutions still taking shape in the late 1800s. Considerable capital investment had built the nation's infrastructure and huge flows of immigrants had fueled the industrial growth machine. Immigrants needed to learn a strange language, assimilate into an unfamiliar culture, and prepare for work in an entirely new Industrial Age.

America stayed out of the European war but sympathies for the Allies grew; in 1917, the United States finally, though reluctantly, entered World War I. The war brought substantial government intervention into the American free-market economy, including increased regulation and the takeover of key industries such as the railroads. At the end of the war, the United States held back from joining the emerging world order—the League of Nations—and retreated into isolationism and protectionism. Citizens turned their back on the "outside world" and focused completely on America. Ours was an insular view of the outside world with the belief that two great oceans protected us.

From 1921 to 1936

It was boom times during an era of laissez-faire (or lenient capitalism) in the American urban economy in the early 1920s, and with the growing industrialism came the emergence and the rise of the large modern corporation. America still practiced protectionism in its foreign trade and isolationism in its foreign affairs. Gradually, U.S. investment in capital goods (factories and products) spread around the world. Unfortunately, the U.S. farmer did not share in such good times and an agricultural recession eventually turned to a deep depression.

The period saw the booming U.S. stock market revealed as a bubble overblown by increased speculation and unsustainable real estate and construction investments; the bubble burst. The 1929 crash brought down the U.S. banking system and destroyed unprotected individual savings. Unemployment, food lines, and general despair tarnished the laissez-faire philosophy of previous years and threatened to discredit capitalism itself.

Socialism saw its strongest growth during this period and such unrest had wide repercussions throughout the United States and around the globe. Educators had their own approach to further organizing their own labors; students and teachers continued to be highly regimented.

To heal the Great Depression, Franklin Roosevelt's New Deal fostered a massive, comprehensive transformation program of American society and its economy, all of which was carried out at breakneck speed. This was the period when the foundations of modern industrial regulations, financial markets, and social policies were put into place. Short-term measures helped to shore up a weakened economy by putting millions of jobless individuals to work and delivering economic recovery through very heavy government intervention.

From 1937 to 1945

Eventually, an economic recovery took hold and so too did another war in Europe. While FDR's political influence was unmatched, he saw great opposition to his policies, particularly in the court system. While some New Deal programs were discontinued as the economy improved, the basic framework of market regulations and social policies was widely accepted.

After the Japanese attacked Pearl Harbor, the United States came into World War II with both fists swinging. The war created an overnight need to rapidly educate and train thousands of men and women to work in our factories. The wartime economy regulated strategic industries; wage and price controls were put into place. FDR gained a third and then a fourth term. Exports boomed as America became the world's "arsenal of democracy," building the machines and munitions of war for our allies, especially Great Britain and Russia. Germany surrendered. After the United States used two atom bombs, the war with Japan also ended. The partition of Europe caused the "an Iron Curtain to descend," to quote Winston Churchill. A fifty-year Cold War was ushered in.

Between 1946 and 1959

After World War II, Harry Truman embraced policies of increasingly centralized government control to expand the U.S. economy through full employment. As the economy stabilized, wartime controls were gradually released. Truman's social liberalism came up against strong dissent in his own party, and the Korean War and the full onset of the Cold War further stoked a growing anticommunist, security-focused sentiment. Republican Dwight D. Eisenhower became president.

Eisenhower used a cautious form of government intervention with steady but unspectacular economic growth results. The anticommunist hysteria of the McCarthy era faded, and a groundswell of civil rights protests grew across the South. Expanded homeownership, public housing, a rush to the suburbs, and major highway programs transformed the U.S. economy and geography in ways that endure to this day.

The Sixties

John F. Kennedy brought an uplifting sense of aspiration into public life in 1960, but his legislative impact fell far short of the enthusiasm he raised. JFK used government policies to deficit spend, to spark higher employment, and to accelerate economic growth. The civil rights movement came to the fore for mainstream America in 1963. It was during this period that the disciplined classroom behavior of teachers and students rapidly began unraveling in the local school. Teachers seeking to better relate to students substituted "relationships" for traditional classroom discipline. The "Camelot" era collapsed abruptly and violently with Kennedy's assassination.

Lyndon Johnson's administration tackled both "guns and butter" issues at the same time. First came the War on Poverty, then increased social opportunities, and with it the striving for greater civil rights. During this period, the most sweeping civil rights legislation since Reconstruction was passed and the local school was placed squarely in the center of "righting" the 150 years of social wrongs of an entire nation.

American commitment to the Vietnam War deepened, and so did its opposition. Increasing unrest in the South and the inner cities sparked a rise of violent protest movements and counterculture, and such activities spilled over into the local school classroom. Children emulated protests seen on TV with increasingly outrageous behavior.[3]

Teachers decided to dress down in the classroom in a vain attempt to better relate with students. Moral relativism took center stage, justifying almost any social cause and further setting the stage for plausible denial as the explanation of too many unacceptable actions. In a year marked by assassinations and upheavals, Johnson withdrew from the 1968 presidential race; Richard Nixon was elected.

From 1969 to 1980

Between 1969 and 1980, the U.S. economy ran out of steam and inflation took hold, soon compounded by the first oil shock. Nixon's wage and price controls failed to tame inflation. Amid continuing social upheaval, Nixon was caught in the Watergate scandal, and the ensuing investigation led to his impeachment and resignation. The Vietnam War wound down but left deep scars, especially in the schools as old-line classroom teachers found it more difficult to cope with increasing student unrest. Newer teachers were woefully ill prepared for the challenges of a new world classroom.

The brief Ford administration was powerless to control inflation and soon unemployment rose as well, signaling the exhaustion of government-controlled economic policies. The Carter administration faced the nation's most serious energy crisis and mounting foreign policy challenges. A protracted hostage crisis at the U.S. embassy in Iran compounded the national malaise and finally undermined the Carter presidency. In schools, the students believed that "anything goes" as both behavior deteriorated and student performance declined. In spite of all their best efforts, the teachers rapidly lost control.

The Eighties

The beginning of the decade ushered in the "Reagan revolution," bringing tax cuts and reduction of government size through spending cuts and more delegation of power to the states. Tight monetary policy tamed inflation, and growth resumed again. The shift to lower taxes and fiscal discipline proved lasting. Reagan's personal charisma boosted national pride, but new social crises were mounting. The Berlin Wall came down and brought with it a new era in free-market global capitalism. It left the United States as the sole global superpower with special obligations and challenges in a rapidly changing world. Japan's economy prospered and increasingly dragged American business and government into a more competitive free-market global economy.

After a series of political and financial scandals, a U.S. recession took hold, revealing new social inequalities and placing even sharper focus on the skyrocketing federal deficit and national debt. Despite the end of the Cold War and the Gulf campaign, the George H. W. Bush administration stumbled on its economic policy. A promise to focus on improving the economy helped propel Bill Clinton to the presidency.

1993 to the Present

Bill Clinton began with some early missteps, but scored major achievements with rapid deficit reduction through spending cuts and tax increases. In the process, he lost his majority in Congress. The U.S. economy boomed and America regained its luster and participation in the global economy. Rapid improvements in technology and the explosion of the Internet transformed the economy and shepherded in the Knowledge and Information Age. The changes hit the American schoolroom and the workforce, catching both by surprise and virtually ill prepared for a knowledge economy.

The deficit was erased but Clinton was tarnished by personal scandals. George W. Bush became president in the controversial 2000 election arbitrated by the U.S. Supreme Court. While deteriorating performance of American schools remained high on the public's mind, Bush rapidly passed tax cuts to gain political points as the boom ended and a mild recession set in.

The projected surplus shriveled rapidly as the free-market global economy moved forward. But on September 11, 2001, terrorists attacked the physical and political landscape of the United States to unsettle our domestic economic policy and introduced a new array of uncertainties. Defense and security spending increased and increased again. Eighteen months later, the U.S. invaded Iraq.

The economy sputtered as the recession showed signs of a gradual but uncertain recovery. Corporate corruption scandals rocked the confidence of America.

School legislation passed in 2002 aimed at strengthening school, teacher, and student accountability, but the new money and new thinking needed to back up new school accountability goals became increasingly scarce. The uncertainty of the nation's security took center stage in each state and locale.

WHERE DOES THIS LEAVE THE LOCAL SCHOOL?

First, the changes in social and economic norms shifted rapidly and dramatically over the last half of the twentieth century. The post–World War II "back to norms" dramatically unseated by the space race in the 1950s, the social unrest stemming from political assassinations and an unpopular war in the 1960s, a search for new direction in the 1970s, student and teacher behavioral changes in the 1980s, and the prosperity of the 1990s took our eye off the ball of the future and education.

Second, the new world order (or, more properly, disorder) changed domestic priorities and pointed to widespread budget crises for the foreseeable future. State and local government budgets fell under heavy financial burden. The G. W. Bush promise of "Leave No Child Behind" can be expected to lack the kind of monetary support needed by financially strapped local school districts.

Third, if more money could improve local school performance, then we would have been well along the way to universal success a long time ago. State and local taxes have poured billions of dollars into local school districts for twenty years; dropout rates over the corresponding time period, as one measure of results, have only worsened. High school graduation rates have long remained at around 70 percent and the readiness of students entering the workforce has never been more dismal.

Less than a year following September 11, 2001, seventeen states face reductions in their budgets for K–12 schools and twenty-nine face cuts for their university systems. The gap between the reality and the political rhetoric about raising standards in local schools is widening. For example:

- Massachusetts cut 10 percent across the board—$320 million from its school budgets.
- Tennessee cut back its $15 million gifted program for its most talented and challenging students.
- New Jersey asked the courts for relief from an $83 million obligation in extra state money to repair buildings, hire teachers, and improve instruction.

Local schools and school districts must now find innovative and creative ways to do a tougher job better, in a time of slumping revenues. Washington is going its own way, running up deficits and borrowing from Social Security, while the states and their local schools are falling deeper into a jam.

A CRISIS OF HIGHER U.S. DROPOUT RATES

A study of high school graduation rates reported in *School Reform News* revealed the seriousness of the school dropout problem.[4] It showed an appalling "one in four U.S. students (26 percent) did not finish high school in 1998, with the rates soaring to almost two out of four for blacks (44 percent) and Latinos (46 percent)."

The failure rates in many urban districts were even higher, with almost three out of four students (72 percent) in Cleveland, Ohio, quitting school without a high school diploma. Not surprisingly, the pressure for giving parents school vouchers for greater school choice got its start in Cleveland.

When a participant at a March 2001 education conference in Washington, D.C., asked why so little attention was being paid to the alarmingly high dropout rate among African Americans and why the U.S. Department of Education (USDoE) reported incomplete and even inaccurate dropout statistics, an aide to President George W. Bush replied: "The truth hurts, and few people want to share the truth about underperforming students these days."

Six months earlier, Kaleem Caire, president and CEO of the Black Alliance for Educational Options (BAEO), asked the authors of a US-DoE dropout study issued during the Clinton administration why it had overstated the number of African American children receiving high school diplomas. It was explained that, in addition to students who actually graduated from high school, the data included recipients of so-called high school equivalency diplomas. Then, referring to the controversial "wall chart" once displayed at USDoE, they said the federal government stopped reporting on the number of ninth graders who completed high school in four years because it painted "too bad a picture of productivity of the nation's public schools." Such anecdotes explain why BAEO commissioned the study *High School Graduation Rates in the United States*.[5]

Parents and other taxpayers need accurate information about the educational status of the nation's children. BAEO determined it was time to examine honestly the effectiveness of our nation's schools and the educational achievement of our children. BAEO, as do others, knows that a high-quality education is our children's primary passport to achieving their life's goals as adults.

> Until many more . . . minority students . . . are very successful educationally, it will be virtually impossible to integrate our society's institutions completely, especially at leadership levels. Without such progress, the United States also will continue to be unable to draw on the full range of talents in our population during an era when the value of an educated citizenry has never been greater.[6]

The study shows how official dropout numbers paint a picture far rosier than reality. The BAEO study exposes in shocking detail just how abysmal graduation rates are in some major American cities, particularly for black and Latino students.

High School Graduation Rates

BAEO study author and Manhattan Institute scholar Jay P. Greene computed a national graduation rate for the class of 1998 of 74 percent, a number significantly lower than the national high school completion rate of 86 percent reported by the National Center for Education Statistics (NCES), an arm of the U.S. Department of Education. Most recently, NCES reported the 2001 graduation rate had inched up to 86.5 percent.

Why the gap between the BAEO and NCES figures?

- Greene explained the NCES numbers are inflated partly because the federal agency counts persons who receive General Educational Development (GED) or alternative certificates as full high school graduates, even though they acquire those certificates after quitting high school.
- The study found NCES data flawed because it relies on self-reporting of educational status. Since that requires people to admit they are high school dropouts, its results are more likely to seriously undercount dropouts.
- The study calculated graduation rates by a method both simpler and more likely to depict the true successes or failures of public school systems by tracking students moving into or out of an area during that five-year period.

The most revealing findings were even wider disparities among major urban areas, states, and racial/ethnic groups. Five of the nation's fifty largest school districts had graduation rates below 50 percent.

- Cleveland was in the cellar, with just 28 percent of its students finishing high school.
- The next lowest graduation-rate group of cities were Memphis (42 percent), Milwaukee (43 percent), Columbus (45 percent), and Chicago (47 percent).

The large school districts with the highest graduation rates were Fairfax County, Virginia (87 percent); Montgomery County, Maryland (85 percent); Albuquerque, New Mexico (83 percent); Boston (82 percent); Jordan, Utah (80 percent); and Virginia Beach, Virginia (80 percent).

A state-by-state look at the data was also not particularly flattering:

- Georgia had the lowest overall graduation rate in the country, 57 percent.
- Tennessee was next at 59 percent.
- Mississippi and the District of Columbia tied at 60 percent.
- Georgia and Tennessee were also among the states where fewer than half of black students graduated high school.

Some Anomalies

The study also unearthed these intriguing irregularities:

- Some states with the best overall graduation rates had the worst rates for African Americans.
  - Wisconsin had the second-best overall graduation rate (87 percent) and the worst graduation rate for African Americans (40 percent).
  - Minnesota had the second-worst African American graduation rate (43 percent) but one of the highest overall graduating rates (82 percent).
- Nationally, the graduation rate for African American students was 56 percent.
  - West Virginia had the highest graduation rate for African Americans (71 percent).
  - Massachusetts (70 percent), Arkansas (67 percent), and New Jersey (66 percent) followed.
- Nationally, the graduation rate for Latinos was 54 percent.
  - The lowest-scoring states in this category were Georgia (32 percent), Alabama (33 percent), Tennessee (38 percent), North Carolina (38 percent), Nevada (40 percent), Oregon (43 percent), Colorado (47 percent), and Arkansas (48 percent).

Montana had the highest graduation rate for Latino students (82 percent), a statistic that needs to be tempered by the fact that Montana has

34

few Latino students. Perhaps the best performers in this category were
Maryland and Louisiana, each with 70 percent graduation rates for
Latinos.

School Dropout Reports

Greene offered some scornful commentary on school bureaucratic
use of "event dropouts"—the students who leave school within one year
of having been registered in the particular school—to issue dropout reports. In order to look good, central offices often assumed children
moved out of town or followed some route other than dropping out of
school, such as home-schooling or pursuing a GED.

That method results in implausible reports, such as one from the Dallas Independent School District claiming an annual graduation rate of
98.7 percent. The BAEO study, by contrast, showed Dallas graduation
rate is just 52 percent.

Greene asked, "If only 1.3 percent of students drop out each year,
how is it that Dallas had 9,924 students in eighth grade in 1993 but only
5,659 graduates in 1998, while the total student population in the district went up by 10.5 percent?" There is simply no other reasonable explanation for several thousand missing students than that they dropped
out, "making the 1.3 percent event dropout rate simply unbelievable."

More a Matter of Reality than Data

The NCES needs to vastly improve the quality of its data on high
school completion, a key measure of educational quality. The federal
government annually spends $40 million for the National Assessment of
Educational Progress, which the NCES uses to document student ac-
quisition of knowledge. It spends less than $1 million to collect and
measure dropout/high school completion statistics.

A look at the real world our children are preparing for comes down to
this: Children who do not earn a high school diploma, much less a college degree, will have a much more difficult time achieving the American dream. It all comes down to the fact that fundamental changes are
needed in our local schools to increase classroom and student accountability.

NOTES

1. Understanding Attitudes about School-to-Career, *Jobs for the Future*, 1997.

2. The Freeman Institute, 1103 Burkhardt Lane, Severn, Maryland.

3. One amusing incident comes to mind. About this time period, one of my children asserted to my father, "You know what you have, Grandpa? You have Grandpa Power! You and all the other Grandpas can get together and demand what you want."

4. *School Reform News* (January 2002).

5. Black Alliance for Educational Options, *High School Graduation Rates in the United States* (2002).

6. "Reaching the Top," introduction to *High School Graduation Rates in the United States (2002)* by the College Board (1999), commissioned by the BAEO.

3

NEW STANDARDS OF COMPETITIVENESS

Eighty-five percent of those polled rate schools that provide school-based and work-based learning, career options information, and career training as "good" or "very good."[1]

—Public Perceptions and Opinions, 1997

ECONOMIC PERSPECTIVE

Opponents of greater U.S. participation in the global economy tend to promote fear of what such a policy would entail. They repeatedly cite a potential loss of jobs, empty factories, or bread and soup lines circa 1929. Most recently, they've added the war on terrorism to the warnings.

On the other hand, supporters of this new form of vigorous competition look forward to the challenge of the free-market global economy with the confidence and with the judgment that the United States can not only gain the lead in the global economy but also help shape its future.

There are consequences if we proceed deeper into the global economy as well as consequences if we do not go forward faster. The message will either be that America, the only remaining global superpower, is up to the economic challenges of the twenty-first century or that America is losing its vision. The choice that confronts us today is certain to impact generations of American to come. Whatever option we choose, it sends a clear message to the global village.

Participation in the global economy is not a one-shot deal nor is it a decision made at a single point in history. It is an ongoing process, with pivotal choices made years or even decades apart. It calls for international cooperation and zealous competitive participation. It is our best hope for creating new world-class paying jobs for Americans.

It means investing in the future to bring about increased national wealth. Such wealth is primarily now generated by human capital— from knowledge and skills—and it flows from the most culturally diverse and *potentially* best-schooled, best-trained, and most productive workforce in the world.

Knowledge and learning is the "rationing" system that determines the financial rewards and personal security in the American workplace. Our capacity to launch an armada of workers with upgraded knowledge and thinking skills adds up to our gross national intellectual capital. The promise of strengthening and growing our economy flows directly from the total amount of national thinking skill we can put together.

In a free-market global economy, a nation's borders are not guarded walls; instead, they are more like bridges to encourage cooperation and partnership. In a complex, information-rich world, no nation can "go it alone" because each is part of an interdependent economic whole. So, too, each person needs to learn and relearn how to carry his or her own "bucket of water" in such a constantly changing economic environment.

America has two missions in this global economic environment: to continually seek and uncover opportunities to lead and to link with ventures and enterprises of different nations.

The European Community (EC) formed its Common Market and now, after several years, has issued the Eurodollar, a uniform currency. NAFTA (North American Free Trade Alliance) spawned a free-trade North American continent where tri-nation enterprises and their workers cooperate and (at other times) compete. SEATA (South East Asian Trade Alliance) was organized into a regional trading bloc in response to the EC and NAFTA. Africa is now in the process of putting together a continent-wide economic development organization.

Such changes in global business alliances and relationships eventually hit home to affect every American business, every American city, and every American worker. No longer can a manager count on the status quo to plan ahead. New products and multiple plant locations drive manufacturing. Each worker needs to view the global dynamics of the day and the dynamic changes as a whole new ball game with new rules. What holds the American worker back from seeing and better understanding the new situation?

FREE-MARKET GLOBAL ECONOMY

Schools need to better prepare American students to thrive in a free market but an uncertain workplace. Stressing the need for the local school to learn more about the needs of its local business enterprises allows a window through which the teachers can catch a view of these new dynamics. The relentlessly competitive nature of free markets and the need for students to prepare in only a few short years are their challenges to make it in a dynamic economic environment.

Such red flags about global job competitiveness may not help motivate educators to change their view of the quality of teaching delivered in the classroom, but the fact remains—and continues to loom— that every student needs to be brought along to be a productive entity.

Today's students need personal initiative to improve their learning. This is the heart of helping children see why they are prodded to get up in the morning, brush their teeth, clean up, eat breakfast, and catch the bus to school. For example:

- The music student has the ambition to be an artist, musician, or singer.
- The student-athlete knows practice leads to college or the pros.
- The science student sees that medicine deals with changing knowledge.

- The civics student views the law as part of an ever-changing world.
- The business student stays abreast of changing trends and markets.
- The auto tech student knows high tech now helps tune car or truck systems.
- The student nurse uses new knowledge in patient care or medical assisting.
- The student paralegal is the professional knowledge alter ego to the attorney.
- The student environmentalist copes with changing Earth and climate patterns.
- The law enforcement student looks for new forms of security threats.
- The firefighter student learns modern buildings are complex systems.
- The student teacher adapts daily to more demanding standards.
- And on and on.

The student in each of these examples comes to see how such an education leads directly to a future of individual wealth. In the uncertain world of a free-market economy, each of us comes to learn what it means to be a lifelong learner. To help grasp the meaning and value of these global free-market ideas, we reach back two centuries.

ADAM SMITH'S VIEW OF ECONOMIC GROWTH

In 1776, Adam Smith published *Inquiry into the Nature and Causes of the Wealth of Nations,* adding a second revolution to that year. On the New World side of the Atlantic Ocean, a political democracy was born. On the other side, an economic blueprint for generations to come was offered. His vision became the eyeglass prescription for future generations, including our own.

Following *The Wealth of Nations,* men began seeing the world around them with new eyes; they saw how the work they did fit into the whole of society, and saw that society as a whole was moving inexorably toward a far-off but clearly visible goal. In a word, Smith brought a new vision into being. The new vision was not a state but a system—more precisely, a "System of Perfect Liberty" to set forth a blueprint for a new form of social organization—what we call economics.[2]

The Laws of the Market

Smith's blueprint solutions center on understanding two key problems:

- How does a society hang together? How is it possible that a community in which everyone is busily following his or her own self-interest does not fly apart?
- What guides each individual's private activities (school or otherwise) so that it conforms to the needs of the group? Without any central plan, how does society manage to get those tasks done that are necessary for survival?

From these fundamental questions, Smith formulated the laws of the market. What he was looking for was "the invisible hand," as he called it; where "the private interests and passions of men" are led in the direction that "is most agreeable to the interest of the whole society."[3]

Knowledge is repeatedly seen as the invisible hand of wealth distribution. This simply means that *it takes knowledge and skills to gain a well-paying job in a knowledge economy*. Without the requisite knowledge and skills, Smith's blueprint relegates one to the bottom rung of the ladder. It is as cruelly simple as that.

The other question is: What about society? The laws of the market are like the laws that explain how a spinning top stays upright; but there is also the question of whether the top, by virtue of its spinning, will be moved along the table.

To Smith, and to the economists who followed him, society is not a static achievement of mankind that goes on reproducing itself, unchanging from one generation to the next. On the contrary, society is an *organism* that has its own life history of change. In this sense, *learn* is another word for change.

Smith's laws of the market are simple: Certain kinds of behaviors in certain social frameworks will cause foreseeable results. Thus, there are few true surprises. Specifically, he shows us how individual self-interest operating in an environment of similarly motivated individuals results in competition, and how competition generates the goods and services that society wants, in the quantities that society wishes, and at the prices society is prepared to pay.

Self-interest only drives men to action; something else prevents the pushing of profit-hungry individuals from holding society up to exorbitant ransom: *competition*, the conflict among the self-interested players in the marketplace. A person who allows his self-interest to run away eventually finds that competitors slip in to take away his business. Thus, interaction tempers selfish motives to yield the most unexpected result: social harmony.

The laws of the market do more than impose a competitive price on products and services. These laws also see to it that the producers of society respond to society's demands for the quantities of goods it wants.

For example, suppose we decide we want more bikes than are being turned out, and fewer cars. Accordingly, we will scramble for the stock of bikes on the market, while the car factories grind to a slow pace. As a result, bike prices tend to rise, and car prices tend to fall. (Even special deals and TV promotions cannot endlessly generate the need for another car.) As bike prices rise, profits in the bike industry also rise; as car prices fall, profits in car manufacturing slump.

Here's where self-interest steps in to rebalance supply and demand. Workers are soon laid off from car factories as they cut production; the workers then move to the bike business where they are needed and where business is booming. The result is obvious: Bike production rises and car production falls further. The reverse is also true.

Through the mechanism of the free market, we, as consumers, change the allocation of elements of production to fit our new desires. (We need a bike but we do not need a car.) Yet no one issues an order, and no government authority establishes a schedule of output. Self-interest and competition, solely acting one against the other, accomplish this transition.

There is also one final accomplishment. As the market regulates both prices and quantities of goods according to consumer demand, so also does it regulate the incomes of those who cooperate to produce such goods. In other words, if profits in one line of business are too large (say, bikes), other businessmen rush to enter that field and produce even more bikes until competition has lowered the surpluses. And if wages get out of line in one kind of work, there will be a shift of workers into the favored occupation until it pays no more than comparable jobs with that same degree of skill and training.

Also, if profits or wages are too low in one trade area, there will be an exit of capital (money) and labor (workers) until the supply better adjusts to the demand.

All this may seem somewhat elementary, but consider what Smith had uncovered in the mechanism of the market: a *self-regulating system* for society to provide for its citizens in an orderly way. It's like a room thermostat that automatically controls the flow of warm or cool air into the room according to the occupants' desired comfort level.

Does the world really work this way? To a great extent, it did, in Smith's day. Business was competitive, the average factory was small, prices did rise and fall as demand ebbed and flowed, and changes in prices did bring into play changes in output and occupation.

How about today? The nature of markets has changed since the eighteenth century. We now have lots factories making both bikes and cars. Today's market mechanism is characterized by the huge size of its players: giant corporations that produce hundreds of thousands of cars and bikes and that operate globally. And today, strong labor unions do not behave as though they were individual proprietors and workers. Their very size enables them to stand out against the pressures of competition, to disregard price signals, and to consider what their self-interest shall be in the long run rather than in the immediate press of each day's buying and selling. A union strikes as the last straw in trying to reach for its workers' needs.

These factors have weakened the guiding function of the free-market mechanism to some degree, but for today's teacher and student the critical message is this: "For all the attributes of a modern-day economic society, the great forces of self-interest and competition, no matter how watered down or hedged about, still provide basic rules of human and economic behavior that no participant in a market system can afford to disregard entirely."[4]

We live in a different world than did Adam Smith but the laws of the market are still very detectable today and still determine how it affects us today and tomorrow, if we just stop for a moment to examine its operations. "No society can surely be flourishing and happy, of which by far the greater part of the numbers are poor and miserable," wrote Smith. Not only did he have the boldness to make such a radical statement more than two centuries ago, he went on to demonstrate that society was, in fact, constantly improving; that it was being propelled, regardless, toward a positive goal. It did not move because someone willed it to, or because the English Parliament or the American Congress might pass laws, or because England or America won a battle. It is this fact: *An economic society moves because there is a concealed dynamic beneath the surface of things that powers the social whole like an enormous engine.* This hidden dynamic is what needs to be communicated to the student. Smith saw the tremendous gains in productivity that sprang from the small division and specialization of labor. Smith was impressed enough with the specialization in a small factory of ten people to write about it. Imagine what he would have thought of a factory employing ten thousand!

Smith's great gift of the division of labor lies in recognizing its capacity to increase the universal wealth that reached to the lowest ranks of the people. In eighteenth-century England, the people at the lowest ranks received little of the universal wealth and led a pretty grim existence. But viewed in its historical context, it is clear that—cruel as that existence was—it meant a considerable advance in society.

So what drives society and an economy to multiply wealth? Partly, it is the market mechanism that harnesses the creative powers of a man or woman in a setting that encourages him or her, even forces him or her, to invent, innovate, expand, and take risks. This is one of the major benefits of lifelong learning (change).

Two other pressures buried deep beneath the surface of the restless free-market activity drive the market system in a rising spiral of productivity.

To Smith, workers, like any other commodity, could be produced according to the demand. If wages were high, the number of workers would multiply; if wages fell, the numbers of workers would decrease. Smith put it bluntly: "the demand for men, like that for any other commodity, necessarily regulates the production of men."

In the mid-1950s, America witnessed the movement of almost all textile plants out of New York and New England and into North and South Carolina in search of less-costly labor. And in less than fifty years, we again witnessed American textile factories moving out of this country to Malaysia, India, and Mexico, to name just a few, for precisely the same reasons.

Smith did not describe the business cycle. Rather, he saw it as a long fifty-year process or wave, a secular evolution. And it is wonderfully certain. A Russian economist Nikolai Kondratieff formalized this economic theory in the 1920s as a fifty- to sixty-five-year cycle resulting from changes in technologies—from the horse and plow, to man and the machine, to man and the extension of his brain, the computer. Today, we see the implication of each stage of the theory more clearly in the evolution of the American economy and society, having evolved from an agricultural age to an industrial age and now in an information age and next evolving to a full-fledged free-market global economy.

The Economic Role of Government as Smith Sees It

Smith's book took hold slowly and it was not until 1800 that his work achieved full recognition. By that time, it had gone through nine English editions and had found its way to the mainland of Europe and to America. Its critics came from an unexpected quarter. They were the rising capitalist class attacked for its "greed." All this was ignored in favor of the larger point that Smith made in his inquiry: Let the market alone.

In Smith's free and unregulated market, the rising industrialists found the theoretical justification they needed to block the first governmental attempts to remedy the scandalous conditions of the times. Smith's theory unquestionably leads to a doctrine of laissez-faire. To Adam Smith, the least government is the best; governments are spendthrift, irresponsible, and unproductive—but he was not necessarily opposed to government action that has the promotion of the general welfare as its goal.

Smith stresses three things that government should do in a society of natural liberty:

- Protect that society against "the violence and invasion" of other societies.
- Provide an "exact administration of justice" for all citizens.
- Erect and maintain those public institutions and those public works

that benefit the great society but that "are of such a nature that the profit could never repay the expense to any individual or small number of individuals."

In today's world, Smith would recognize the need for strong national defense, a fair and independent judiciary, and the value of public investment for projects too vast to be undertaken by the private sector; he mentioned roads and education as two examples.

Smith is against the meddling of government in a free-market mechanism. He is against restraints on imports and bounties on exports (now one of the prime issues surrounding global trade), against governmental laws that shelter industry from competition (such as steel import tariffs recently enacted), and against governmental spending for unproductive ends (what we call pork-barrel spending). Such governmental activities work against the proper functioning of the market system.

Smith never had to face the problem of whether the government weakens or strengthens the free-market system when it steps in with welfare legislation, which would cause such intellectual agony for later generations.

The importance of exploring Adam Smith in such depth here is this: The advent and spread of free-market global capitalism into more and more nations on every continent changes the competitive ground rules to be faced by today's students in their roles as tomorrow's workers and family members. Today, his theories enjoy wider support and acceptance than ever in both American political parties and around the globe. The difference in acceptance between the Democrats and Republicans remains a matter of degree. Each argues: To what extent should each of Smith's precepts be adopted for the national good?

The Danger of Monopoly

The great enemy to Smith's system is not so much government as monopoly in any form. The trouble with such goings-on is they are both morally reprehensible as well as the inevitable consequence of man's self-interest. His concern is that monopoly blocks the fluid working of the free market. Smith recognized and firmly believed that whatever interferes with the market does so only at the expense of the true wealth of the nation.

In a sense, Smith's vision is testimony to the eighteenth-century belief in the inevitable triumph of rationality and order over arbitrariness and chaos. "Don't try to do good," says Smith. "Good emerges as the by-product of selfishness." Ayn Rand's mammoth 1,100-page novel *Atlas Shrugged,* written in the 1930s (now in its thirty-fifth edition), built an entire movement on this identical theme. Its main message may be more relevant today than when written.

Smith was the economist of preindustrial capitalism. He did not live to see the market system threatened by enormous enterprises, or his laws of accumulation and population upset by sociological developments only fifty years off. When Smith lived and wrote, there had not yet been an inventory-driven "business cycle." The world he wrote about actually existed, and his systematization of it provides a brilliant analysis of its expansive tendencies.

It was 150 years later that John Nash, a Princeton mathematician, further defined the self-interest and independent economic actions of persons and companies first introduced by Adam Smith. Nash contributed the economic application of game theory for which he shared a Nobel Prize. Nash's life was the subject of the book and motion picture *A Beautiful Mind.*

The elegance and importance of Nash's theories to our discussion of surviving and succeeding in the uncertain world of global free-market economic trade is significant. He recognized that the action of "winner takes all" only really works in sporting events. The world of business and human relations into which today's K–12 student will one day emerge has both greater cooperative and noncooperative modes of operation than ever before. When both are at play at the same time, it is called coopetition.[5] For example, American cooperative trade with Japan adds up to billions of dollars each year while at the same time, American carmakers and Japanese carmakers vigorously compete for a share of market and which nation's workers gets the jobs. It is a win-win world.

This is just one of many examples of the need for students and teachers to begin the mastery of complex reasoning early in school. The world is full of arbitrary mixtures of common interests and conflicts of interest; this reasoning power is needed in economics as well as in other social problems where many people interact, and there are potential mutual gains from agreements as well as broad or deep conflicts.

The Knowledge Worker

Well after Smith's time, machines of the Industrial Age replaced muscle power. In the transition to today's Knowledge and Information Age, machines now supplement brainpower. Manufacturing in such areas as steel, autos, rubber, and textiles is run today by knowledge-intensive technology. In the newer industries of aerospace, computers, communications, home electronics, pharmaceuticals, and health services, the use of new technologies has grown even more central to output. The worker uses the machine to extended his mind and supplement his physical limitations.

Between 1970 and 1990, approximately 90 percent of all new jobs created in the United States took place in the information-processing and knowledge services areas such as finance, broadcasting, health care, education, law, accounting, data processing, and entertainment. The entire process manufacturing system is now run with computer-aided machines. The infotainment industry is now estimated to be more than a one trillion dollar industry annually.

As more jobs come from information and knowledge services, the information professional—paralegals, nurses, and technicians—increases his or her share of the total workforce. If we add college-educated professionals—lawyers, doctors, security analysts, consultants, accountants, engineers, computer programmers, and college professors—whose work centers on applying knowledge to problem solving, the nature of the workforce shift becomes even more clear.

Why Explain Adam Smith?

The same broad concepts introduced by Smith still govern today's world where K–12 students learn. They will move into this world in but a very few years.

Today, over 200,000 computer engineers from India work in California's Silicon Valley. Physicians from India dot our hospitals. These are resourceful, well-educated, and industrious people drawn to America to take the available high-paying knowledge jobs. Their children come from families who hold twenty-first-century Puritan values—work hard, save, and learn. In a global economy, the jobs can be done from anywhere in the world and beamed to the user by satellite. This is mind power spurred by quality education at its best.

India's huge software and information technology industry, which emerged during the decade of the 1990s, made India the back room and research hub of many of the world's largest corporations.

Thanks to the Internet and satellites, India has been able to connect its millions of educated, English-speaking, low-wage, tech-savvy young people to the world's largest corporations. They live in India, but they design and run the software and systems that now support the world's biggest companies, earning India an unprecedented $60 billion in foreign reserves.

If I lose my luggage on British Airways, the techie who tracks it down is located in India. If my Dell computer has a problem, the techie who walks me through a solution is based in Bangalore, India's Silicon Valley. Indian software giants located in Bangalore now manage back-room operations—accounting, inventory management, billing, accounts receivable, payrolls, credit card approvals—for global firms like Nortel Networks, Reebok, Sony, American Express, and GE Capital.[6]

GE's biggest research center outside the United States is in Bangalore, with 1,700 Indian engineers and scientists. The brain chip for every Nokia cellphone is designed in Bangalore. When I rent a car from Avis online, it's managed from India.

Many studies now show the positive correlation between education and livelihood but if you are an educator reading this, we are preaching to a member of the choir. Two major factors in determining the future earnings in a knowledge economy are the amount of schooling a student completes and the ability to *keep on learning*.

Few kids will grow up to accumulate the kind of wealth Bill Gates did from starting and growing Microsoft. Before the NBA, Michael Jordan honed his basketball and investment skills with a degree from the University of North Carolina. Educators are challenged to find new and innovative ways to raise student expectations about the value of learning now and to embrace a culture of lifetime learning.

The conclusion is inescapable: The more formal education one has, the chances are greater that the more money one can make over a lifetime. Conversely, with few exceptions, those having little formal schooling are practically doomed to economic adversity. Education is not only society's "rationing hand" (to borrow Smith's words) for sharing wealth, it is also the catalyst for creating new wealth.

The free-market global economy has brought us all into an era of human capital—a period in which talent, intelligence, and knowledge are increasingly the essential ingredients for the nation and its citizens to achieve and maintain world-class economic dexterity.

THE GLOBAL MIND-SET

Over the past decade, teachers and school curricula have done a masterful job of bringing students along to view the impacts of a global environment as a system. The Earth's limited air and water supplies, global warming, rare vegetation, threatened species of animals, and the rain forest are just some of the global issues that today's students are now sensitized to.

The developing nations of Southeast Asia, India, Mexico, and Eastern Europe are also portrayed as having poor, exploited, and underpaid workers producing goods for global export, many of which are imported into the United States. Many NAFTA arguments center on whether Mexican citizens can even afford U.S. export goods.

To set the record straight, Western Europe already has a large and established middle-income class and the magnitude of this unprecedented global economic trading opportunity is just beginning to hit home. America's trading history has been built upon the free-market trading system composed of North America, Europe, and Japan. In recent years, Southeast Asia, China, Eastern Europe, Russia, and Latin America have all developed free-market systems. India, with a high-middle class, is in the process of opening its markets to the global economy. At last count, there are an estimated 3 billion persons (and still counting) fully participating in the global economy.

American workers and employers are becoming less surprised about the extent to which our worldwide counterparts are now more prosperous. It's estimated that 10 percent of China's 1.2 billion people (120 million persons or almost half the U.S. population) now own their own homes and have a TV set. Nearly half the people in South Korea, Taiwan, Hong Kong, and Singapore have reached the rung on the middle-class ladder. Thailand, Malaysia, and Indonesia show up to 20 percent of their population headed there as well.

Some American workers, businesspersons, and politicians focus on the negative balance of trade and the stream of goods flowing to the United States. They believe trade negatively impacts domestic competition, holds down wages, and cuts out American jobs.

The local school needs to help revamp any remaining Industrial Age thinking and guide students along the path of readying themselves to be America's future knowledge workers and employers: to prepare for leadership and professionalism in a twenty-first-century global economic renaissance.

CUSTOMER-FOCUSED QUALITY

Too many American organizations still use 1950s thinking to tackle twenty-first-century challenges. Such organizations and leaders have yet to adopt the pioneering path set forth in the global quality movement of the last half century.

Post–World War II management thinking got stuck on standardization, production efficiency, and cost control as the driving forces to achieve profit goals. It placed its highest value on short-term financial results—numbers that, for the most part, are driven by accounting policies and practices to meet the demands of the equity markets. The ENRON, WorldCom, Adelphia, and Xerox debacles are vivid testimony of this view having gotten completely out of hand.

Such managers also saw advertising as the principle tool to promote standard products, manufacturing efficiencies, overhead absorption, and lower output costs. American business turned to advertising, not to better quality, to convince the customer.

On the other hand, successful foreign competitors sharply departed from such tunnel-vision thinking, turning skillfully toward *quality* as the underlying value and driving force for customer satisfaction and profit improvement. These competitors targeted increased market share and long-term customer relationships as carrying the highest value. It viewed step-by-step process improvements and quality at each stage as the ultimate winning appeal of product or service to the customer.

Testimony to the success of this quality strategy is demonstrated in Japan's obsessive commitment to quality in automobile design and production as well as the quality of consumer electronics. More than half the cars and trucks in the *Consumer Reports* 2002 annual recommended new and used vehicles that carry a Japanese label. One glance around a consumer electronics store attests to the market dominance of Japanese consumer electronics.

As the free-market global economy reached wider acceptance, the most successful American companies stepped up to accept quality as the key to increasing its productivity and competitiveness. Such companies recognized that quality builds upon people skills and a company's ability to use highly skilled people to maximum workplace advantage. The most successful companies shifted their mental models to match the terms and conditions of a knowledge economy.

SUDDENLY, A NEW BEGINNING

In his autobiography, retired Chairman of the Joint Chief of Staffs and Secretary of State Colin Powell relates the experience of one day coming to grips with the fact that the Cold War was over. The U.S. game plan of containing communism had been swept away by a single pronouncement from Soviet President Mikhail Gorbachev. Powell tells of the event that after leaning across a conference table and suddenly declaring an end to the Cold War, Mikhail Gorbachev turned to him and said "General, you will have to find yourself a new enemy."

With only a few years to go to retirement, Powell thought to himself that the ground rules that had dictated the balance of power for the previous forty years, and his thirty years of military service, had just flown out the window. With this change came the end of a bipolar world and the entire systems theory of how the world turns.

All at once, the free world more than doubled in size. New markets dramatically opened up. New opportunities for investment were available throughout the old Iron Curtain countries. The new global economy began shifting into higher gear.

To benefit from these changes, it was necessary to have more than merely access to information. What was needed was focused and dynamic information—even more so than capital. Overnight, the new currency of nations became knowledge.

In a knowledge economy, it is nonsense to value the assets of knowledge-based companies like Microsoft as we would an Industrial Age company. Asking three questions helps us grasp the difference:

- How much land and buildings does a Microsoft own and does it really matter?
- How does their physical inventory compare to accumulated brainpower?
- How much office space does each person need to think?

In an Information Age company, the assets walk out the door in the evening inside the heads of the workers. Many even leave in the morning after an all-night session.

NOTES

1. "Public Perceptions and Opinions of the School-to-Work Program," Economic and Issues Research, 1997.

2. Daniel Yergin and Joseph Stanislaw, *The Commanding Heights: The Battle between Government and the Marketplace That Is Remaking the Modern World* (New York: Simon and Schuster, 1998).

3. Yergin and Stanislaw, *The Commanding Heights.*

4. Yergin and Stanislaw, *The Commanding Heights.*

5. Leon M. Lessinger and Allen Salowe, *Game Time: The Educator's Playbook for the New Global Economy* (Lancaster, Penn.: Technomic, 1997).

6. Thomas L. Friedman, "India, Pakistan, and GE," *New York Times* (August 11, 2002).

4

THE LOCAL SCHOOL
NEEDS DIRECTION

High school students in Philadelphia's School-to-Careers programs had higher GPA standings than students not involved.

High school students completing work-based learning in Philadelphia's School-to-Careers programs were 10 percent more likely to attend school (87.5 percent vs. 78.8 percent).

High school students completing work-based learning in Philadelphia's School-to-Careers programs were 12 percent more likely to graduate from high school (86.6 percent vs. 93.6 percent).[1]

—Philadelphia School District Study, 1997

It doesn't make much difference whether we continue building schools further away from urban centers and bus kids to and from farther away if educators are unable to improve the teaching and learning processes taking place inside of the classroom. Quality—not location—is what eventually raises the level of student achievement.

SEARCHING FOR DIRECTION

The U.S. Constitution does not guarantee public education. It is the individual state constitution that provides this guarantee, but it generally contains language so bland as to be only minimally prescriptive. This leaves us with a basic question stemming from prescriptive disputes. It is more a matter of philosophy than of money; this one involves the Constitution, not the checkbook: *What is the minimal obligation of government to educate its children?*

Year after year, states grapple with this question; most come around to seizing on the money issue as far easier to wrestle to the ground than the range of differences in values and beliefs. In June 2002, a New York appeals court ruled that its public schools are obligated by state constitution to do nothing more than prepare students for low-level jobs, for serving on a jury, and for reading campaign literature—the equivalent, the court suggested, of an eighth- or a ninth-grade education.

The appeals court did not argue with the fact that the New York City schools are weighed down by low-paid and undertrained teachers, that classes are too large, that the textbooks are badly out of date, or that classes take place in rundown buildings.

In weighing this sad state of affairs, the court suggested it is not the court's job to set an ideal—or, as the judges termed it, an "aspirational" standard—but to determine what is a constitutional human right to education. No matter how troubled its public schools, the City of New York met that limited standard, despite how low the bar had been set.

Thus, barring a catastrophic collapse in student achievement, the court suggested, it was up to the politicians and the legislature to make the decisions about what kind of education they would accept. And if the citizens were unhappy with the political judgments of the people they had elected, they could vote them out of office.

This ruling came about as a result of New York State having been drawn into a legal battle over whether the state is paying its fair share toward New York City's vast and ailing public school system. Over the years, numerous motions, arguments, and news conferences highlighted the struggle as a typical rhetorical war over money: How much money did the city's schools need? Are the suburbs getting more per student? Who should pay to bring the city's schools up to a higher standard?

As a beacon of direction, many saw the appeals court ruling as an act of wisdom because it recognized that money is not necessarily the cure for an ailing school system. Most education stakeholders by this time have learned that "dollars in" does not equate with "quality out" and that there are other factors at play: poverty, immigration, labor contracts, and so forth. It is yet to be seen whether the State of New York will ultimately have to start imposing higher standards—and start paying for them.

Whatever the outcome, the New York ruling exposed a gaping hole in the debate about what is meant by that state's guarantee of a "sound, basic education" for all its children. The state constitution says only that the state is required to provide "the maintenance and support of a system of free common schools wherein all the children of this state may be educated."

The phrase "sound, basic education" was coined by the New York Court of Appeals, the state's highest court, as an interpretation of what the state constitution required. In 1995, that court decreed that schools must prepare students to "function productively as civic participants capable of voting and serving on a jury."

What does it mean to "function productively" as a citizen? The courts agreed that the requirement meant more than just turning out people who can find their way to courthouses and the voting booth—but beyond that, there were vastly differing views.

- In January 2001, Justice Leland DeGrasse of the New York State Supreme Court in Manhattan emphasized the difficult decisions citizenship can involve this way. "Jurors today must determine questions of fact concerning DNA evidence, statistical analyses, and convoluted financial fraud, to name only three topics." Justice DeGrasse found that the city schools did not prepare students to meet that challenge.
- The appeals court disagreed, contending that "the skills required to enable a person to obtain employment, vote, and serve on a jury are imparted between grades eight and nine, a level of skill which plaintiffs do not dispute is being provided."
- Another question is the career options for which a "sound, basic education" should prepare students. Conceding that schools should not be required to prepare students for an "elite four-year college," Justice DeGrasse ruled that students should be prepared for "competitive employment," meaning something more than "low-level jobs paying the minimum wage."[2]

- To the appeals court, this decision smacked of social engineering. Instead, a student should simply be provided "the ability to get a job, and support oneself, and thereby not be a charge on the public fisc," wrote Justice Alfred D. Lerner for the majority.[3]

In other states, the courts have gone farther than New York in tackling the fundamental question of what the state owes to its poorest communities, and to set a higher standard.

At what point, some courts have asked, does the state legislature have to make decisions that might go beyond the minimum constitutional requirement but that reflect deeper social values?[4]

In neighboring New Jersey, for instance, it was a more expansive view of the state's obligation to its schoolchildren that drove the courts to order the state to equalize the difference in spending (inputs) between school districts with wealthy property tax bases and those with poor ones. The New Jersey Supreme Court took the view that schools should be responsible for remedying educational deficits that might have their roots in larger social problems, like crime and poverty. It did not come to grips with the standards and levels of student performance (outputs and results) expected.

Legal scholars argue that differences among court decisions have more to do with how willing courts are to become involved in offering direction through public policymaking than with interpreting any constitutional mandate. For instance,

- The New Jersey constitution requires "a thorough and efficient system of education," a far less radical scheme than the redistribution of property-tax wealth that has been imposed by its state courts to achieve equality among school districts.
- The California constitution offers poetic language requiring the legislature to "encourage by all suitable means the promotion of intellectual, scientific, moral, and agricultural improvements."
- North Carolina's constitution reads: "Religion, morality, and knowledge being necessary to good government and the happiness of mankind, schools, libraries, and the means of education shall forever be encouraged."

- Florida's constitution was amended in 1998 expanding state guarantees of an "adequate" education to now include an education that was "efficient, safe, secure, and high quality."[5]

In 1989, a Kentucky Supreme Court decision required its schools to fulfill seven educational goals, including grounding in the arts; the ability to make informed choices about economic, social, and political systems; and preparation for advanced training in academic and vocational fields. As a result, Kentucky overhauled its educational system and test scores rose significantly. This is considered something of a success story. When viewed in the context of "schools for their time," it is groundbreaking.

The evolution in litigation has overlapped the rise of the educational standards movement, and many courts have used the high school graduation standards developed by their states as benchmarks for what school systems should provide. In contrast to its relatively low threshold of a "sound, basic education," New York State is now phasing in tougher Regents tests in five subjects as part of its graduation standards, though it is not yet clear how much the state will be willing to pay to help implement them.

It is too soon to tell which states will be forced to undertake changes similar to Kentucky's; given the issue's political weight and the huge amounts of money involved, however, it is inevitable that the decision will fall to a state's highest court.

THE GAP BETWEEN THE BUILDING AND CLASSROOM PERFORMANCE

Schools were once an important civic landmark built to last a century. They represented a community investment intended to inspire civic pride and broad social participation in public life. Today, however, too many newer schools resemble big-box warehouses in a "Wal-Mart–type" architecture reflecting little, if any, community pride—and an expected lifespan of thirty years.

The big-box warehouse also accurately reflects what happens within too many schools. We have been reminded that K–12 education has been operated as a production-line operation since the onset of the Industrial Revolution; following World War II, the local school used Industrial Age thinking to turn out Industrial Age workers, the kinds of workers called for.

The quality of community affects the mind-set that the students bring with them into the classroom. At one time, a strong and cohesive neighborhood offered a safety net and positive outlets for young people. The local school served as the community anchor, meeting the varied needs and interests of parents, children, and educators alike.

A smaller, community-centered school that helps tie together a neighborhood is the kind of school that many educators and parents are calling for again. If a school district tried to build such a school, however, it could not do so in many places. In some areas we could not even renovate or add on to such a school.

Until the 1960s, the neighborhood school was situated on only two acres of land, a site that today is considered "substandard" under many state school architectural policies. Typically, state standards for a new elementary schools call for at least ten acres of land, plus one acre for every 100 students. Much larger sites are the required standard for middle and high schools, but acreage requirements are only one of several public policies that rule out the possibility of retaining—or building new—neighborhood-centered schools.

WHY CHILDREN CAN'T WALK TO SCHOOL

Two factors—size and "community-centeredness"—relate to smaller schools located in the middle of a neighborhood. Some educators have come to believe that larger schools are better because they provide economies of scale (a term straight from the factory floor to the Industrial Age accounting department). These educators also believe large schools offer students more subject offerings and permit more competitive sports teams who can practice on more ball fields (a concept straight from the Industrial Age theories of marketing and product mix). Many other education leaders prefer smaller, community-centered schools.

It is not necessary, or very likely, that we will settle the debate over whether big or small schools are better in order to recognize that many parents, teachers, and education experts across the country say that smaller schools are better for kids, better for learning, and better for communities. Many studies support these empirical observations.[6] Because the larger schools are falling further and further behind in delivering higher levels of student achievement, the size of the school remains a central issue.

Huge schools shroud young people in a "cloak of anonymity," according to the National Association of Secondary School Principals.[7] At the same time, studies find that smaller schools produce better academic results, lower dropout rates, and fewer incidents of student violence. Graduates and students from big schools support this point and it is not hard to see the anecdotal evidence.

At a large school, the student feels like a cog in a machine. The smaller school offers students what metal detectors and guards cannot—the safety and security of being where the students are known well by people who care for them. Interestingly, at a time when teachers and administrators clamor for greater parental involvement, the majority of larger schools are designed to serve as stand-alone instructional facilities where community access is limited and uninviting. Parental involvement in the large school is not discouraged but neither is it particularly encouraged.

Despite the outcry for smaller, community-centered schools, "megaschool sprawl"—giant schools built on the outskirts of town with tenuous connections to the communities they serve—continue to be the norm and continue to spread across the country. So the American icon—the small school that a child could walk to in a neighborhood where he or she knew the neighbors—is fast disappearing, to be displaced by long lines of yellow school buses lined up out front of the megaschool both morning and afternoon.

Only 13 percent of all trips to school are made by walking and bicycling today.[8] Schools that hold the memories of generations are disappearing. And handsome school buildings—the landmarks that used to inspire community pride—are fast being discarded for plain, nondescript structures that resemble warehouses.

This nondescript factory-style school building mirrors what is going on inside the school—K–12 teaching processes that are warehoused on shelves, like a Costco store, and then pulled off and used to move children through the grade-level system. Adding insult to injury, stressful morning and afternoon drives to more and more distant schools at peak traffic hours further separate parents and their children.

Since the 1980s, urban and regional planners in high-growth states like Florida, California, and Texas have focused attention on slowing the proliferation of urban sprawl—the building of housing and shopping centers situated further and further from urban centers. But like the movement of post offices and other public buildings away from downtowns to outlying suburban commercial strips, the migration of the school has moved from settled neighborhoods to "middle-of-nowhere" locations—one more factor that weakens the ties that once brought people together. Like residential and commercial sprawl, "school sprawl" contributes to the dismemberment of the community.

The market for inner-city family housing oftentimes depends on the quality of the inner-city school. According to the Metropolitan Forum Project of Los Angeles and the James Irvine Foundation, "Many residents fleeing the inner city for the suburbs are leaving in search of more stable and dependable schools. One way to help reverse the trend of outward migration is to develop schools in cities and townships that encourage community involvement, achieve academic excellence, and attract more people to live and raise their families there."[9]

Can educators be expected to bring the smaller local school, sometimes still located in downtown, around to deliver an equivalent quality of education and student results as the big-box suburban school? Can educators and education stakeholders—the politicians who really set the expectations for our public schools—concentrate on what it takes to equalize the results for every school classroom wherever it is physically located?

TURNING OUR BACKS ON THE PROBLEM

The issue is not where we build our schools, although this is symptomatic of our view of the problems. The issue is this: How do we bring each school and each classroom up to the quality performance standards necessary to meet the needs of our times?

We know young people need independence. Most students or educators have never heard the term "school sprawl," but they feel its consequences anyway.

Many schools do not have an activity bus because of budget constraints. If a student (who demonstrates interests and initiative) does any sort of after-school activity, she must drive herself, bum a ride, or wait to be picked up. The inconvenience on parents is enormous and the disincentive to children is equally as great.

Given the increasing numbers of single-parent households and two-parent households with neither parent working in close proximity to the home or school, we have systematically created a perfect conundrum of school and social failure. Students and teachers recognize this through their own frustrations.

Parents are worn out from chauffeuring kids, and kids are sick of begging rides in order to go anywhere. Suburbanites are car-dependent. Out there, buses do not run, there is no Metro, there are no trains—no public transportation—and the distances are almost always too far to be easily walked or biked.

As urban sprawl scatters the elements of the community ever more randomly across the landscape, "school sprawl" follows the same pattern, making the spontaneous play among schoolmates mostly a thing of the past. Today, children must be driven miles to play with friends, meaning time-strapped parents spend even more hours on the road carting their children from one place to another. Most mothers average no less than an hour a day just driving their children around.

American adults average seventy-two minutes every day behind the wheel, according to a U.S. Department of Transportation's Personal Transportation Survey. "This is, according to time diary studies, more than . . . twice as much [time] as the average parent spends with the kids," writes Robert Putnam in *Bowling Alone*.[10]

Teenagers often are left little other choice but to take a job to buy a car—or pay for car insurance—if they want to have a social life or engage in after-school activities. While many would agree that young people can benefit from working, excessively long hours at after-school jobs takes time away from homework and physical exercise. It also helps set up the incentive to finally give up on school.

Many communities have been designed to be "car convenient" but not for children. The freedom of children to explore their communities is limited when walking is not safe or enjoyable. Sadly, this deprives neighborhoods of the activity and laughter of children walking and bicycling to and from school together.

The Centers for Disease Control (CDC) have linked several health problems associated with urban sprawl, including the absence of sidewalks in many neighborhoods and the replacement of walking and bicycling by automobile travel for all but the shortest distances. This has contributed to a national obesity epidemic among youngsters.

Physical fitness goals are often used to justify the large and numerous athletic fields that go along with megaschools in outlying locations. The design and layout of new communities make it hard to work simple exercise like walking into one's daily routine. The percentage of overweight children has increased by 63 percent over the past thirty years, according to the CDC, whose research shows that 60 percent of overweight five- to ten-year-old children already have at least one risk factor for heart disease.[11]

So we add the automobile to the school bus as silent contributors interfering with the student's health, then offer the student "fast food" school menus laden with super-sized sugar soft drinks, and submit the child to learning in the big box.

COMMUNITY PLANNING AND SCHOOL PLANNING

Local government typically uses planning, zoning, and other growth management laws to protect the community's quality of life. Through such laws, municipalities and counties try to preserve or create close-knit neighborhoods that permit kids to walk to school. Such laws help assure taxpayer funds are not wasted but rather used to maintain public assets, including those important to young people, like schools, libraries, parks, and recreation centers.

Siting and building a new school in an outlying area either responds to or greatly alters a community's growth patterns. Often, such schools are put there in response to expected demand but in fact serve to establish new beachheads for residential sprawl. New school sites selected by local school districts are often donated by (or, most often, strong-armed from) community developers. This forces a town or county to speed up the construction of new roads, water mains, and sewer lines to the area.

Research into local planning and development activities in Lincoln, Nebraska, prompted W. Cecil Steward, dean of the College of Architecture at the University of Nebraska, to conclude that, "the public school system . . . is the most influential planning entity, either public or private, promoting the prototypical sprawl pattern of American cities." He refers to public school systems as "advance scouts for urban sprawl."[12] Our own community planning and consulting work over a twenty-five-year time period in Florida large-scale community development bears out Steward's conclusions. It shows that a new school is a greater attractor to new residential building and road construction than providing a golf course, shopping center, or a major employment center.

In some states, school districts are either exempt from local planning and zoning laws or they simply ignore them.

Florida, a bellwether state for local government comprehensive planning, took more than twenty years from the passage of its mandatory local comprehensive planning act to include planning for local schools. School superintendents and school boards regularly ignore or bypass local master land-use plans, capital improvement plans, and local zoning in siting and operating a new school facility. It's as though the school has no relationship, no link, to its community, its economic vitality, and its land-use planning.

Under California law, public schools can be located without regard to local plans intended to promote orderly, well-planned growth. New schools are often built on productive farmland located outside urban growth boundaries. Such schools require the extension of city services outside of the designated urban service areas and violate state growth management policies intended to prevent sprawl.

On the other hand, South Carolina passed a law in 1994 requiring local planning agencies to plan for growth in their respective jurisdictions.[13] However, if a local school district's plan conflicted with a local comprehensive plan—for example, if a proposed school site fell outside a jurisdiction's urban growth boundary—no government authority could stop the project, even if the location makes no sense to the community, according to the South Carolina Coastal Conservation League.[14] "Local [school] districts are not obligated to work with local planners or other government officials on selecting a new site," says the league, "and they need not ensure that its location fits into a community's overall comprehensive plan."[15]

In California, the rift between school planning and general community planning became so intense that sponsored legislation in 2002 addressed the problem, as had Florida during the previous year. Such laws require school districts to defer to local zoning in jurisdictions that have local comprehensive plans, provided these plans contain provisions to accommodate the need to build or renovate public schools.

California school districts exempt themselves from local land-use regulations with a two-thirds vote of the school board. Florida's mandatory compliance with local concurrency laws demands that school construction plans must statistically correspond with available or planned roads, water, and sewer facilities.

In short, most school districts still may, if they so choose, ignore plans for sensible, well-managed, smart, and responsible economic growth in their communities and region. Rather than supporting responsible growth management, schools act as magnets for further sprawl and increase their dependence on school busing, thus further contributing to a growing broad-based economic crisis.

COORDINATING SCHOOL FACILITIES AND COMMUNITY PLANNING

Maine has emerged as a leader in promoting better communication and coordination between school facility planners and general community planners.

The state's Department of Education encourages school superintendents to contact the State Planning Office (SPO) staff before making decisions about where to build new schools. Such contacts enable SPO staff to arrange meetings with local school planners for the purpose of coordinating school facility planning and local planning.

Through these contacts, superintendents are better informed about the community's plans for new growth and development, and they are encouraged to take these plans into account. Following SPO site visits and meetings, the SPO staff makes recommendations to the state education board regarding the merits of state financial assistance for local school projects. The board is not required to accept these recommendations, but it often does.

In a model of interdepartmental coordination, the Maine State Planning Office and State Board of Education recently collaborated on the publication of a brochure designed to help local officials make better school siting decisions. Entitled "The ABC's of School Site Selection," the brochure urges school districts to:

- Avoid sprawl; consider school renovations or expansions in central locations whenever possible;
- Analyze school sites for their proximity to village centers and established neighborhoods; and
- Select sites served by adequate roads, utilities, and other essential services.

The brochure gives real-life examples of schools that have followed these principles.

Schools are part of the glue that holds older neighborhoods together. Darrell Rudd, president-elect of the National Association of Elementary School Principals put it this way, "You take out the school, and that's the beginning of the decline of the neighborhood. You've got to have a school to have a neighborhood."

The school introduces people who would otherwise remain strangers to each other. In so doing, it helps build a sense of community, which is central to solving society's bigger challenges, education included.

Conversely, the removal of a long-standing, community-centered school can and does dishearten an older neighborhood—precisely because they have seen firsthand the effects of boarded-up schools on other older neighborhoods after citizens in those places raised an uproar over the closing of historic neighborhood schools.

The school system should make it easier for parents, educators, and community residents to preserve and renovate historic neighborhood schools when it is feasible to adapt these buildings for modern educational programs. When it isn't, communities should be able to build well-designed new schools *in the same neighborhood* without undue damage to surrounding homes. Above all, the rules should not put pressure on communities to replace historic neighborhood schools with megaschool sprawl in remote locations.

Maine and Maryland are demonstrating that state policies can help bring education and "smart growth" goals together. School boards in Boise, Idaho, and Evansville, Indiana, are demonstrating the benefits of good stewardship to education and community preservation. Citizens in

Durham, North Carolina, and Atchison, Kansas, are showing that they can successfully mobilize to save older and historic schools that are threatened.

The central message is this: Political leadership needs to lead and direct the performance of the local school, its teachers, and its students to be brought up to the standards demanded by a twenty-first-century global workplace that is expected to be laden with increasing uncertainty for years to come.

NOTES

1. Philadelphia School District Study, 1997
2. Robert F. Worth and Anemona Hartocollis, "Johnny Can Read, but Well Enough to Vote?" *New York Times*, June 30, 2002.
3. Worth and Hartocollis, *New York Times*.
4. Worth and Hartocollis, *New York Times*.
5. Worth and Hartocollis, *New York Times*.
6. A good source of research and debate on this subject can be found at www.DesignShare.com.
7. *Breaking Ranks: Changing an American Institution: A Report of the National Association of Secondary School Principals in partnership with the Carnegie Foundation for the Advancement of Teaching on the High School of the Twenty-First Century* (Reston, Va.: National Association of Secondary School Principals, 1996), 46.
8. *Kidswalk-to-School: A Guide to Promote Walking to School*, Centers for Disease Control and Prevention, U.S. Dept. of Health and Human Services, p.1.
9. *What If: New Schools, Better Neighborhoods, More Livable Communities* (Los Angeles, Calif.: Metropolitan Forum Project of Los Angeles and the James Irvine Foundation), 19–20.
10. Robert Putnam, *Bowling Alone: The Collapse and Revival of American Community* (New York: Simon and Schuster, 2000), 212.
11. *Kidswalk-to-School*, 1. See also *Journal of the American Medical Association* (October 27, 1999) and *Journal of the American Medical Association* (October 17, 1999).
12. W. Cecil Steward, "Case 13: Lincoln, Nebraska, Public School Systems: The Advance Scouts for Urban Sprawl" in *Under the Blade: The Conversion of*

Agricultural Landscapes, edited by Richard K. Olson and Thomas A. Lyson. (Boulder, Colo.: Westview Press, 1999), 370.

13. Local Government Comprehensive Planning Enabling Act, S.C. Code Sections 6-29-310 through 6-29-1200, 1994.

14. Christopher Kouri, "Wait for the Bus: How Lowcountry School Site Selection and Design Deter Walking to School and Contribute to Urban Sprawl," *South Carolina Coastal Conservation League* (November 1999), 2.

15. "Wait for the Bus," vi.

5

INITIATIVES FOR LOCAL SCHOOL IMPROVEMENT

Graduates of Boston's Pro-Tech [STW] initiative were 16 percent more likely to attend college in the year following graduation than the national average (87 percent vs. 62 percent).
African American graduates of Boston's Pro-Tech [STW] initiative were 26 percent more likely to attend college in the year following graduation than a comparison group of nonparticipants (79 percent vs. 53 percent).[1]

—*Jobs for the Future*, 1998

Different states give us some innovative benchmarks for improving local school practices. Many initiatives come from the private sector. Some changes seep out from state education departments. Few, if any, initiatives seem to originate from the local general-purpose government.

LOCAL AND STATE INITIATIVES

Tennessee Links to Baldrige

The Tennessee School Improvement Planning process links to the Baldrige National Quality Program. Tennessee requires school improvement plans to be submitted to the Tennessee Department of

Education for approval every two years using the total quality management (TQM) process.

The Baldrige builds on the TQM process by specifically supplementing it with education program criteria. These provide tools for school organizations to improve their planning and operational processes. Baldrige, whether used in a business, a government agency, a health care organization, or a local school, provides practical quality tools for use by such organizations to strive for continuous improvement and performance excellence.

Tennessee Quality was chartered in 1993 by the Tennessee Department of Economic and Community Development to help the organizations of the state achieve performance excellence using the Baldrige criteria for assessment and evaluation. To date, over 700 organizations in Tennessee have made use of the Tennessee Quality Process.

Most other states, forty-four at last count, have similar affiliated organizations to support the use of Baldrige criteria in their states. Tennessee Quality has multiple levels of recognition, which allows all organizations to participate and learn. The most prestigious, the Tennessee Quality Excellence Award (TQA) is earned by organizations that meet strenuous criteria demonstrating significant accomplishments.[2]

Clarkson University, New York, Partners with Local School Districts

A Lasting Business/Educational Partnership Program has long been underway by Clarkson's Michael Ensby, of the Interdisciplinary Engineering and Management Department. Since 1993, Clarkson has partnered with local school districts and area companies to provide meaningful hands-on opportunities for students to develop quality management competencies, such as teamwork, problem solving, and project management, while introducing them to the concept of social entrepreneurship.

Student mentors receive a comprehensive introduction to the tools of quality and project management while they plan and execute their yearlong project with a local school system requiring the use of those tools. This program has become a benchmark in the New York state educational system, winning the 2000 New York State Tech Prep Partnership Award.

Benchmarking the Clarkson program helps the local community learn how to structure educational–business partnerships, to master the application of quality and project management tools in an educational setting, and to understand the value of aligning objectives in multistakeholder partnerships.

Honda of America Partners with Educators

The Honda Education Outreach program works with educators in fifteen Ohio counties, covering an area of 6,731 square miles. Additionally, they are involved in quality activities in thirty-nine schools/districts.

The Honda Partners Program includes K–12, junior vocational schools, educational service centers, and alternative schools. Such experiences demonstrate classrooms initiatives, how educators can partner with business, what resources are available from businesses to educators, and how to introduce quality into the classrooms

Ohio Educators Partner with Other Educators

The Ohio Learning First Alliance, a statewide collaborative project as a partnership of Ohio's major educational organizations, assists Ohio school districts with improved student learning. Its first three-year project, funded by the Jennings Foundation, involved the implementation of systemwide academic content standards in ten local school districts through the avenues of state/local collaborative leadership, community partnership, family engagement, and aligned educational and instructional practice. This holistic, partnership-driven approach is expected to increase public involvement in education, align practices, and improve student learning.

By benchmarking the Ohio collaborative, local school leaders come to understand the benefits of working through an educational collaborative to enhance learning, to identify learning tools and techniques to align educational partners in support of learning, and to discover methods for developing and sustaining a collaborative in its own local school or district.

Maryland Links Baldrige with Education

Maryland State Superintendent of Schools Nancy S. Grasmick helped make the Maryland State Department of Education (MSDE) and the state's local school systems more efficient by linking the MSDE and six local systems to participate in the Baldrige in Education Initiative.

MSDE and the local school systems in six counties will begin adopting some of the best education practices as spelled out in the Baldrige initiative. Maryland is one of six states selected through a competitive process to participate in the program that is a national partnership of twenty-four business and education organizations managed by the National Alliance of Business (NAB) and the American Productivity and Quality Center (APQC).

Under Ronald Reagan, Congress created the Malcolm Baldrige National Quality Award to recognize the best practices from some of America's high-performing companies and share those ideas among the business community. In 1999, the Baldrige Quality Program was expanded to better serve healthcare and school systems.

"There are countless ways school systems can apply Baldrige Criteria to operate more efficiently. In turn, this will help increase the achievements of school reform by maximizing our resources" said Dr. Grasmick. "Baldrige is all about taking the high ideals developed in boardrooms and turning them into performance excellence in the classroom. That is exactly what we have aimed to accomplish in Maryland schools."

The Baldrige program helps align state and local education programs through consistent strategies that focus on setting goals, tracking progress, and achieving continuous improvements over time. The initiative helps develop opportunities for business and education leaders to forge long-term local partnerships.

The driving force behind Maryland's involvement in the Baldrige Education Initiative was the Coalition to Promote Excellence in Public Education in Maryland. That group drew representatives from MSDE, the Maryland Center for Quality and Productivity, the Maryland State Teacher's Association, the Maryland Association of Boards of Education, the Maryland Secondary School Principals Association, the Maryland Business Roundtable for Education, the Maryland Congress of Parents and Teachers, the Governor's Workforce Investment Board, several higher education institutions, local school districts, and key business leaders.

North Carolina Links Schools to a Growing Job Market

North Carolina has a positive climate for job growth. The state is challenged to ensure that workers have the higher-level skills required for jobs of the future, the very jobs that require workers to continually think, learn, and work smarter.

JobReady, the North Carolina school-to-work system, is a partnership between business, government, and educators to help young people prepare to meet the demands of this state's changing economy. Partnerships are developed locally to address the needs of communities and the public schools of North Carolina and the state's community colleges are active in this effort.

The role of the local school in JobReady is to prepare students for careers by showing the relevance of education to the workplace and by helping students develop skills to be successful. The process begins in kindergarten and continues through postsecondary education. More specifically:

- In elementary school, students are introduced to careers through career-day events or guest speakers.
- Middle school students start to explore possible careers through activities such as job shadowing with someone in the workplace and career exploration courses.
- High school students are asked to choose a broad-based career major by the tenth grade, in order to select courses that will help prepare them for that career.
- Before graduation, students participate in a work-based learning experience such as job shadowing, internships, apprenticeships, or cooperative education. Course work is rigorous, and students are held accountable through regular assessments.

Teachers and counselors actively engage in professional development to learn more about other professions and careers. Such experiences include summer internships or job shadowing activities in business or industry. Teachers then may work together to develop integrated lesson plans based on what they have seen in business and industry.

Employers help in developing curriculum for the schools and by providing work-based learning experiences for students and educators.

Across the state, local partnerships are eligible for planning and implementation grants through JobReady.

Canada Links with an American Idea

Canadians have successfully spread quality principles, tools, and techniques throughout their school systems. There is no magic in the answer. It comes from just sound practices fuelled by the passion to help children become self-motivated learners, problem solvers, and team players.

The Ottawa community organized for growth and took steps to sustain the enthusiasm of teachers, parents, businesspeople, and most important, the children. They knew from the outset that quality enhances the learning process, and now they are proving it.

TEACHER BACKLASH TO CUT THE LINKS

Repeatedly, we're asked "How can we get everyone on board to implement school reform?" The answer, to be perfectly honest, is "You won't."

Right off the bat, we estimate and have learned that a third of teachers welcome change, another third will choose to sit on the fence to see which way the winds of change are likely to blow, and the other third will simply resist change, ask for transfers, or drop out of teaching altogether.

To see this theory in recent actual practice, twenty teachers at one of Philadelphia's schools that had been contracted to be managed by Edison Schools Inc. requested transfers to different schools for the fall 2002, according to teacher's union officials.

Officials at for-profit Edison and the School Reform Commission encourage "teachers to stay and be a part of reform, to wait and see what good things come to their schools," said a spokeswoman for the School Reform Commission.

But Philadelphia Federation of Teachers (PFT) officials said teachers at Luis Munoz-Marin School are reacting to citywide "chaos" created by the reform commission's plans and say more upheaval is coming. Some 416 Philadelphia schoolteachers planned to retire in June 2002. "We have a lot of teacher vacancies now, and we are going to have a greater number," warned the PFT.

PFT President Ted Kirsch said one of the plan's methods—reconstitution—has already failed here, and that the commission made its decisions without consulting teachers or parents.

Reconstitution is a "bottoms-up" overhaul of a district, school by school. San Francisco pioneered reconstitution in 1984 under court order. A districtwide committee of teachers and administrators was directed to classify each school as exemplary, satisfactory, or nonperforming. Nonperforming schools were to be required to file a plan that spelled out their goals and vision. The city was to provide those schools with additional staff development programs. At nonperforming schools, teachers were to reach consensus to approve the plan. Creating consensus and motivating staff were the most important elements in turning a school around.

The new plan gave teachers one year to agree on a plan and improve curriculum. Teachers who did not stick to the plan were to be "involuntarily transferred." Some details remained to be worked out, such as how to identify teachers who don't work with the plan and how voluntary and involuntary transfers are to be carried out, but the teachers' union won a major concession from the district in that no teachers would be forced to leave their school. When San Francisco reconstituted its first four schools in 1984, the district spent six months planning their curriculum and locating talented, veteran teachers. The concentration of energy and effort and intelligence did bring about some measurable improvement according to the AFT, but in most of the schools reconstituted since 1993, inexperienced staff members were thrown together with inexperienced leadership.

In Philadelphia, PFT warned the reform commission against trying to change the union's contract before it expires in August 2004. "I assure you that the PFT will take whatever action is necessary to enforce the provisions of our contract and to enforce good learning conditions for our students," said Kirsch. He declined to discuss specific actions.

Edison, which at the time was having its own financial problems, continued talks with the union as soon as the commission authorized it to do so, said an Edison spokesman. "We have great relationships in many of our schools where there are collective bargaining agreements," he said. "We think that can be possible in Philadelphia." With Edison in financial difficulty and stress running high in Philadelphia, it is uncertain how this change initiative will develop.

THE MISSING LINKS IN THE LOCAL SCHOOL

"The most American thing about America is its public school system," said twice-presidential candidate Adlai Stevenson. For 200 years, the public school has been a center of community interest, bringing people together—the daughter of the banker, the son of the farmer, the children of factory workers and sharecroppers—on common ground, where they come to know one another as American citizens.

Unfortunately, we only need to look back at the chronologies of the public schools and the U.S. economy presented earlier to identify how the local school has first been tossed this way and then tossed that way in response to waves of change.

Public schools have repeatedly been the fierce battleground for the struggles of changing ideas and values. Alabama Governor George Wallace stood in the doorway of Birmingham High School to defy the bayonets and orders of the federal government to desegregate. Arkansas Governor Orville Faubus propped himself squarely in the doorway of Little Rock High School to defy the president and attorney general of the United States. The University of Mississippi was forced at the point of a bayonet to admit James Meredith, its first black student, whose own son freely chose to attend Ole Miss in 2002.

Many of America's most contentious debates—over freedom of religious expression, evolution, and segregation, to name a few—have taken place within the public school system. The Scopes Monkey Trial pit William Jennings Bryan, Bible in hand, against Clarence Darrow, with Darwin's *Origin of Species* in hand, and debated the teaching of the theory of evolution in a Tennessee public school classroom.

So it comes as little surprise that Americans today are still sharply divided on whether public schools are effective and the role they are intended to serve. The local public school is in deeper trouble today because grim stories appear daily in the media relating school violence, increasing dropout rates, and poor school and classroom performance.

Critics deride the public school as inefficient, bureaucratic, and coercive. In 2002, the U.S. Supreme Court in a split 5–4 decision ruled that parents dissatisfied with the performance of their local school could receive a voucher to help pay for their child to attend a religious-based school. Thus, the grand experiment continues, but always at the expense of the children who need a better education.

Even among proponents of the local public school, there is an uneasy sense that schools have lost their way.

One reason Americans feel like schools have lost their way is that we have forgotten where we've been. The barrage of criticism and defense of public schooling has left little space for deliberating what unites us as well as divides us, what part broad civic goals have played within a pluralistic society, what traditions are worth preserving, and how education has or has not adapted to the remarkable pluralism of America.

A Theory of Action

Student achievement gains in Canton and Stark County, Ohio, have been due in large measure to a sustained, concentrated, and collaborative instructional effort among seventeen school districts. Instructional leaders, together with representatives of a local school–business–foundation partnership and with a national consultant, Robert Kronley, put together a theory of action explaining why change is needed and how it occurs.

The theory does not prescribe solutions. It spells out benchmarks for the community on why and how change is taking place in their schools. This approach helps local leaders gain new knowledge on developing a theory of action, to view new dimensions of public/private collaboration, and to better understand a new framework for capacity building.

Sound familiar?

INITIATIVES LINKING INDUSTRIES AND LEARNING

The Utility Business Education Coalition (UBEC) is a national, CEO-driven alliance assembled by the nation's leading electric and natural gas utility companies. By teaming CEOs and their companies with local resources, UBEC produces bottom-line results for local businesses and local schools. This is a long-term commitment by corporate partners to improve student achievement, position students for future success in the workplace, and transform community workforce development initiatives.

UBEC measures its success by business success. Its goal is to make sure that communities are making progress so that students slated to graduate in the next two to eight years (today's middle and high school students) have the skills needed for economic and personal success. Through a site-tailored strategic process, UBEC makes sure that investments in people pay dividends.

UBEC works for employers. It knows business issues. UBEC is a reliable partner created *by and for* business. It has worked with company leaders across the country to establish community partnerships that work. UBEC has helped companies assess needs positions, develop strategies, and pursue corporate goals.

UBEC is a one-stop shop by providing companies with the support needed to plan, manage, and evaluate community partnerships. Senior managers rely on UBEC to help them successfully tackle the challenges of managing and evaluating business–education partnerships and setting priorities for their investments in education and workforce development. From assessment to communications, UBEC helps companies reach their goals by:

- Identifying opportunities and assessing links between community and school programs, partnerships, and outcomes. UBEC works with the company, community, and school leaders to set priorities, assess goals, reconfigure resources, and increase student achievement in their communities.
- Building local alliances to help facilitate local strategic partnerships to sustain effective community 501(c)(3) organizations. These new or reconfigured nonprofit organizations focus on school improvement to achieve results and sustain continuous improvements.
- Connecting best practices and benchmarks to provide the most effective community-based education and workforce development practices from around the country.
- Measuring results through gathering information and providing the expertise to measure achievement and monitor progress. The results promote ongoing improvement and deliver a return on the community's investment.

Taking this approach a step further, the National Skills Standards Board (NSSB) initiates scores of certification programs through "a voluntary national system of skills standards, assessments, and certification that will enhance the ability of the U.S. workforce to compete effectively in the global economy."[3] The NSSB, created in 1994, is a unique coalition of leaders from business, labor, employees, education, and community and civil rights organizations. The skills defined by NSSB are being identified by industry in full partnership with labor and civil rights and community-based organizations. The standards are to be based on high-performance work and will be portable across industry sectors.

NSSB has categorized the workforce into the following fifteen industry sectors:

- Agriculture, forestry, and fishing
- Business and administrative services
- Construction
- Education and training
- Finance and insurance
- Health and human services
- Manufacturing, installation, and repair
- Mining
- Public administration, legal and protective services
- Restaurants, lodging, hospitality and tourism, and amusement and recreation
- Retail trade, wholesale trade, real estate, and personal services
- Scientific and technical services
- Telecommunications, computers, arts and entertainment, and information
- Transportation
- Utilities, environmental and waste management

Members from each industry sector come together to form voluntary partnerships under guidance of the NSSB. The partnerships are responsible for developing skill standards, assessments, and certification for their respective industry sectors. Industry skill standards have been widely developed in the manufacturing and the sales and service industry sectors and may be accessed through the NSSM website.[4]

Standards development is underway in the education and training, hospitality and tourism, information and communication technologies, and public administration, legal, and protective services industry sectors.

NSSB is also benchmarking the U.S. system at the international level to help ensure that it is world class. In the past several years, leaders from Brazil, Chile, Germany, Korea, Mexico, Singapore, the United Kingdom, and several other nations have visited the NSSB with the intent of sharing their progress and to learn more about the NSSB system and development plans. In this way, these countries might benefit from and apply NSSB research and experiences in the development of their own skill standards systems.

To keep up to date with NSSB progress, the reader can check out NSSB online, which contains the most extensive collection of skills-related information on the Internet. The site also hosts an electronic version of the NSSB Clearinghouse, housing more than 1,400 skills-related documents; a categorized system of 200 links to domestic and international skills-certification sites; and detailed information on all industry coalitions. Also available at the website is a list of NSSB partners in the national skill-standards system, which can be linked to from the NSSB homepage by simply clicking on the logos for each voluntary partnership found at the bottom of the website page.

LINKING PARENTS TO THE LOCAL SCHOOL

"The dog ate my homework" stands in a long line of student traditions of hiding report cards from parents and telling tall tales about test scores.

New technology is giving parents unprecedented access to their children's school lives; over the next few years, parents will be able to log onto a website to see how their children scored on the big algebra test, or if they turned in their geography assignments last week or, for that matter, if they were even *in* school last week.

The increased monitoring will undoubtedly bring many advantages. Not only will diligent parents be saved from unpleasant surprises around report-card time, but students monitoring their own progress should be able to better balance their studies. Officials say teachers will also be able to record grades and test scores more efficiently with the new software, eliminating the need for regular grade books.

Some teachers are nervous about the new technology and suggest that a parent with too much information is not necessarily a good thing. And the move to up-to-date online information also means an end to thousands of creative excuses and alibis spun for decades about homework and absences.

Even if tall tales fall flat now, students agree that online grade books do have their benefits. Boys and girls now watch their grades closely: One might monitors his or her own grades twice a week; another might log on after every test.

Students already seem nervous. A front-page article in *Tiger Pause*, the student newspaper at Martin County (Florida) High School, announced the new arrival of this technology with this: "One of the worst fears that a student could face is to come home and realize that their parents already know that they failed a test. Now this horrible fear could become a reality with the new Pinnacle online grading system."

The consensus seems to be that it is just a matter of time before every skipped gym class and every missing Spanish homework assignment is laid bare for parental scrutiny. A middle school student might conclude, "You end up getting grounded more."

NOTES

1. Jobs for the Future and the Boston Private Industry Council Survey, 1998.

2. For more detailed application of quality principles to your local school see Allen Salowe and Leon Lessinger, *Healing Public Schools* (2001); *Solutions: Tools and Strategies for Schools* (2002); and *The Solutions Fieldbook* (2002), all available from Scarecrow Education Press in Lanham, Md.

3. The National Skills Standards Board can be found at www.nssb.org.

4. National Skills Standards Board, www.nssb.org.

6

PARTNERING: SMOOTHING THE TRANSITION

Students participating in New York School-to-Work initiatives were more frequently exposed to higher quality jobs involving problem-solving, use imagination and creativity, and working on teams than their non-involved peers (54 percent vs. 41 percent for solving problems; 47 percent vs. 24 percent for using creativity; 56 percent vs. 49 percent for working on teams).[1]

—Westchester Institute for Human Services Research, 1998

About two-thirds of respondents from Tennessee believe that fewer teenagers would drop out of school if schools provided more career education.[2]

—Tennessee Attitudes toward the Workplace, 1998

Thirty years ago, the term "school to work" (STW) was meant to deal with making the transition from high school to the workplace.

Today, in a far-reaching and highly competitive free-market global economy racked with uncertainty, making the swing from classroom to career is anything but smooth. It is a lifelong commitment.

LINKING CLASSROOM TO CAREER

According to a U.S. Department of Education (USDoE) study, 89 percent of the jobs created in the United States between 1992 and 2000 required college-level math and reading skills—but only half of all students entering the workforce brought with them the skills needed to perform these jobs. And when we throw in the fact that that 30 percent of seventeen-year-olds do not complete their high school studies, it shines a bright light on the fact that the nation as a whole is woefully ill prepared, based on knowledge and skill requirements, to successfully compete in the uncertain environment of the twenty-first-century free-market global economy.

Other studies sponsored by government and private industry conclude that too many students coming out of America's schools have poor academic skills, dysfunctional work habits, and inadequate occupational training. This widens the gap between the poor quality of education that too many students receive and the skills they need in the modern workplace.

This situation has given many employers a deep case of heartburn. It has helped motivate employers to take more direct action in shaping the future workforce.

The USDoE defines a school-to-work program as a partnership between businesses, labor, government, education, and community organizations that helps prepare students for the high-wage, high-skill careers of an increasingly global economy.

Although such programs differ from community to community, they all have three core goals: First, to provide students with a relevant education by allowing them to explore different careers and see what skills are needed in today's workplace.

Second, to provide job skills through structured training and work-based learning experiences.

Third, to provide recognized credentials for students by establishing work, education, and training standards that seek to ensure they receive a proper education.

Many employers still ask why they should get involved in school-to-work programs. The short answer to this is: Employers are investing in their own future.

Many students coming out of a U.S. high school today cannot pass the simple spelling test that typical hiring companies give to all job candidates. This type of job candidate increasingly concerns employers.

Is this because our schools encourage "best-guess" spelling and our students learn to depend on spell and grammar checkers on their computers? And how many of our children learn to use a calculator before becoming competent in basic math skills (addition, subtraction, multiplication, and division)? The philosophy of logic is reserved for advanced classes, so many children never learn to give directions in a coherent manner. Many employers feel that today's high school students are in danger of developing lazy thought patterns, and this is borne out when these same students apply for skilled jobs.

PUTTING CLASSROOM-TO-CAREER PROGRAMS INTO PRACTICE

"One thing I have learned from only fourteen months in Washington is that you can pass laws, but the passing of the law really is the easiest part," says Robert Reich, Secretary of Labor for Clinton. "The hardest part is getting it implemented, getting the private sector, educators, and businesses actively engaged in making a law meaningful—breathing life into a law."

We use *classroom to career* (CTC) to describe the scope of this effort. First, the student is being prepared in the classroom. Second, the student is taking his or her first step on a lifelong career; no matter what the first job is, its experience will stay with the student forever.

The challenge is daunting because the commitments required to run a successful CTC effort require each program to have a work-based learning component and a planned curriculum of job training. Workplace mentors, instructional workplace competencies, and a broad variety of other elements are also included. These are performance criteria, not a cookie-cutter approach.

CTC goes well beyond what had previously been asked of employers. If it is to succeed, it will take hundreds of actively involved employers. It will mean linking responsibility for creating opportunities in every community. This involvement will need to occur in a fundamentally different partnership among local business, local government, and local educators.

STUDENTS SHOW THE WAY

At the start of the 2000–2001 school year, Bill Kurth Jr. was enrolled in Mrs. Sue Tracy's creative thinking class with a mixture of sixth- through eighth-grade students at Trafalgar Middle School in Cape Coral, Florida. Mrs. Tracy specializes in teaching this and other classes involving problem solving and creative thinking.

A little more than a quarter of the way through the school year, Mrs. Tracy and her classes were moved to a very small and tight classroom, causing the students to abort the activities that they had previously participated in. One student suggested that the class and its activities should move outside where there was enough room. Then, following suit, another student suggested that they should build an outdoor classroom.

Mrs. Tracy liked the idea enough that she presented it to the principal to see what he thought of it. He liked the class idea and encouraged its construction. The class split into three committees: the design committee (which Bill was in), the communications committee, and the presentation committee. The design committee was responsible for designing the outdoor classroom.

Each of the committee's five members sketched out a design of what they thought the general design appearance and function should include as well as some of its features. After each student drew a design, the student presented his concept to the other classmates. The entire class then brainstormed what the "classroom" should look like and what features to keep. Bill's design was chosen, after which Bill drew another copy of the new design for the class.

For short periods of time, while one committee was idle, the students would help the other groups. After researching the requirements of different local building codes, Bill modified the design once more.

Following this process, the class sent the design to a family member of one of the students who made a computerized blueprint of the proposed structure. Later in the process, the class submitted the drawings to a local construction company that had volunteered to cooperate in the project to approve the drawings and make final copies.

While design-construct review was taking place, the communications committee was writing letters to the school board regarding rules and regulations and then to local companies asking for their cooperation and donations. They also wrote to local building officials regarding the code and regulations so the appropriate permits could be issued for construction. The committee also wrote letters and e-mails to everyone, keeping them updated on their progress.

Lastly, the presentation committee gathered up all the information to be presented to all of the participants and interested groups. Eventually, after a long period of awaiting permits and such, the class got its authorization to proceed.

During the planning and permitting process, Aubuchon Homes, a local homebuilder whose owner was the father of a Trafalgar student, sent an employee, also the father of a student, to help the class. He provided all of the resources necessary and helped along the way.

Bill wasn't there during the year when the classroom pavilion was completed, but he received recognition at the eighth-grade graduation for his special contribution to the achievement of this important education project. All of the costs were donated, but if it had been purchased, it would probably have cost several thousand dollars.

We asked Bill what he had learned from this classroom experience and he e-mailed us: "I think we all learned a little of how the world works and some of the processes and procedures required for building anything. Also we learned how to communicate better with people and it should help us later on in life."

A NEW APPROACH TO LEARNING

Old-line thinking has it that schools and training are distinct enterprises and separated somehow by walls. What does the word "education" bring to mind?

- Education is for kids?
- Education is books, blackboards, and classrooms?
- Higher education is for the top slice of our population?

Training takes on a separate category altogether in the popular thinking. This is something we provide to people who have not received higher education. We train young men and women and then send them on their way. To retrain them is something different again; retraining is reserved for those unlucky few who have lost jobs and now have to get new ones.

The picture that comes out of this is less a system than a collection of loosely adjoined kingdoms with high walls, causing each to barely know that the other exists. These kingdoms confront educators at a time when the central feature of an uncertain free-market global economy is the capacity to tear down walls of every kind.

The flick of a computer key sends information and capital racing through cyberspace, across national boundaries, right through walls of all sorts, to a computer, then elsewhere up to a satellite, and on to a computer in another nation. This is powerful stuff.

At the end of the Cold War, the walls that separated command-and-control economies and free-market economies came down together, opening up new markets for the West and new opportunities for the East. Even the wall between goods and services fell.

We used to know, we thought, what manufactured items meant and what services meant. That wall fell within America's domestic economy as more and more of the value of a product becomes embedded in related delivered services before it is manufactured in terms of planning, product and market research, design engineering, manufacturing engineering, styling, and so forth, as well as services after it is sold in terms of sales, marketing, delivery, and technical support. The modern automobile industry is a prime example.

In this new "boundaryless" economy, what a student eventually earns depends in large measure on what the student learns and then relearns. Many of our best companies have dynamically responded to change by tearing down artificial barriers and by creating in its place teams of people. So, too, must the local school get rid of artificial boundaries.

We, teachers and stakeholders alike, can no longer afford to think of education as something that happens to someone once, something that someone does just when he or she is young. Learning is not an event; it is a *work in process*. It does not happen; it *continues*. It does not start and stop; *it goes on and on and on throughout one's lifetime*.

A system where K–12 schooling, higher education, and skills training are segmented from one another can no longer meet the dynamic needs of an ever-changing American economy or American workforce. The heart of the new economic agenda is to revitalize, restructure, and integrate distinct segments of our society into a system of lifelong learning that constantly and repeatedly builds the skills of American workers. This is good for American workers. This is good for American business.

THE EMPLOYER'S ROLE

Employers play a critical role in building the working components of the classroom-to-career initiative. First, business leaders become full partners in planning and developing CTC opportunities at the local level. It is not enough to have state or federal legislation in hopes of "willing it" to happen.

Next, employers need to sponsor work-based learning experiences for students. Whether it is a fifteen-person tool and die shop, a hospital with hundreds of employees and professionals, or a Baby Bell employing tens of thousands of workers, it takes the commitment of such employers to provide real learning opportunities for young people.

Some of the most successful CTC models are based on employers who, on average, work with only two or three students defining skill requirements, developing work-based learning curricula, providing work experience, and actively supporting and mentoring those students.

For instance, in York, Pennsylvania, a very small tool and die operation with three or four employees provides work-based learning tied closely to school-based learning. The same thing is going on in Vermont, in Kansas, and throughout the South in isolated communities and in individual companies.

Local employers work with local educators to coordinate what is happening at the work site with what students and teachers are doing in the classroom. Research has shown that integrating classroom learning and on-the-job experience yields better results for students who may not learn best in a structured classroom setting.

Such a student learns to love geometry because he learns it in the morning and then goes out and applies it in the afternoon while building a homeless shelter. The student sees the direct relationship between what he is learning in the classroom and what he is building.

Employers are increasingly getting involved in their respective industry's efforts to develop the voluntary industry-led skills standards and certifications provided for by the NSSB, some of which were introduced in the previous chapter. We see this happening across the country with HVAC (heating, ventilating, and air conditioning) contractors, auto mechanics and technicians, retailers, hospital and healthcare workers, hospitality and restaurant workers, to name only a few of the industries involved.

For the student, the advantage lies in completing such a program of work and study and receiving the industry-recognized credentials. It immediately opens up a world of opportunity. The credentials are completely portable. And because it is a voluntary credential that is industry recognized, it allows any potential employer to know that this young person has *earned* these credentials and has *demonstrated* the capacity to continue learning.

In Philadelphia

What started ten years earlier with a few students in a manufacturing apprenticeship has grown in 2001 to a districtwide CTC program in which hundreds of Philadelphia area employers work with thousands of local students and teachers to provide work-based learning experiences.

A high school student spends part of her day at a medical laboratory, a law firm, or a bank. The teacher completes an "externship" over the summer, spending time at local businesses to learn what skills the local employers are looking for in new workers. With strong backing from education officials and a host of corporate leaders, the 200,000-plus student district has made CTC programs a centerpiece of its school improvement strategy.

"For us, school-to-work became the vehicle for engaging employers in schools and really changing instructional practices," said Mary Jane Clancy, the executive director of the education-for-employment office of the Philadelphia public schools. "You can't forget this is about increasing access for students who have not had access. For the first time, our children are sitting in the boardroom—not cleaning the boardroom."[3] The need to raise academic standards (and correspondingly better results) in America's high schools helps put increased pressure on such initiatives. They engage the student by making his learning more hands-on and meaningful. These programs help connect what the student learns in her academic subjects with the knowledge and skills picked up from career-oriented studies and on-the-job experiences in school-related internships.

While some say the classroom-to-career approach has not achieved widespread national success, programs such as the one in Philadelphia are cited as examples of the significant contribution that work-based learning can make. We need to remember that school-to-work (STW) or classroom-to-career (CTC) initiatives always involve a local community and employer teaming with the local school to better prepare the student to compete in a free-market global workplace.

"We should continue to push for alternatives to the very traditional high school classroom that is organized around lectures," said Thomas Bailey, president of the Institute for Education and the Economy in New York City. "School-to-work has been very useful for people to realize that combining the theoretical and the practical has a lot of exciting potential."[4] The classroom-to-career initiative has drawn criticism in some quarters; opponents argue that it amounts to creating job tracks for students. Advocates, on the other hand, see the potential for bridging the gulf between what is or is not happening in the classroom and the skills business leaders insist high school graduates routinely lack. Hopes are especially high for reaching students from minority groups and poor families who drop out of high school at higher rates than their white and middle-class peers.

While U.S. business leaders struggle to find highly skilled graduates amid the economic worries of a new century, many look to CTC programs as this country's version of the successful career education and apprenticeship programs in countries such as Germany and Japan. The movement has also drawn in part on the best practices of vocational and technical education.

In 1994, Clinton signed the School-to-Work Opportunities Act, which led to federal grants totaling more than $1.6 billion in seed money to support programs that included internships, career academies, and job shadowing.

In 2001, the school-to-work movement reached a crossroads when a new administration in Washington made it a lower priority than school vouchers, religious schools, and federally mandated school accountability. With federal funding slated to end, states worked feverishly to keep alive some 1,500 local programs that many educators and employers credit with making academics more relevant for students and increasing business involvement in schools. Twenty-four states also introduced legislation related to maintaining school-to-work programs. Out of the sixty-two bills introduced in those states, about half passed, according to the Denver-based National Conference of State Legislatures.

Career Moves

A report released in February 2001 by the Institute for Education and the Economy at Teachers College, Columbia University, presented evidence that school-to-work programs help reduce dropout rates, improve student readiness for college, and get good reviews from teachers and business leaders.

The report, "School to Work: Making a Difference in Education," is described as the most comprehensive review to date of research examining such programs' impact.[5] The report analyzed results from more than 100 studies on school-to-work programs.

Career academies—a thirty-year-old model that involves breaking up large schools into learning communities centered on a workplace theme—delivered strong results.

The Manpower Demonstration Research Corp., a nonprofit research organization in New York City, began a ten-year study of career academies in 1993. It found that 32 percent of academically at-risk students who did not attend a career academy dropped out of high school, compared with a 21 percent dropout rate for career-academy students.

While these latest findings do not show improved test scores for career-academy students, they do strongly suggest that these students are as likely to pursue higher education as students on a more traditional college-prep path. In one case, graduates of a California career academy were 40 percent more likely to enroll in a four-year college than other students in the same school district.

The National Alliance of Business, which works to improve student achievement and workforce competitiveness, also helped set up partnerships between schools and businesses. NAB often helps local schools develop curricula that are directly relevant to the workplace. Some computer companies, for example, let high school students earn certification by following programs that feature hands-on training in using technology.

A Federal "Stepchild"

Although the 1994 federal STW law passed with strong backing across political lines, momentum for the initiative faded as Clinton moved on to other education priorities. It has not been heard of since G. W. Bush moved into the White House.

While giving students a better general understanding of the workplace, STW programs have unfortunately not been enough for students to acquire the specific skills that translate into jobs unless they opt to go on to college or specialty school.

In Europe, strong apprenticeship programs have served for years as the model for STW programs here, but this approach has been fairly slow to catch on among U.S. educators who are wary of backing away from the "college-is-for-everyone" message.

STW has yielded some solid, if not spectacular, successes. In *What's Next for School-to-Career?* Kazis and Pennington write that only a few states have successfully used school-to-work programs as part of their broader school improvement strategies.[6] "When you look at the evidence, it is not a knockout punch," Kazis said. "But there is evidence it has done right by schools and kids."

Building on Success

In Maryland, STW efforts are organized under a program called Career Connections, which supports student internships and helps restructure schools around small, career-oriented learning communities. One showcase for this approach is the Eleanor Roosevelt High School in Greenbelt, Maryland.

For years, the science and technology magnet program at the Prince George's County schools attracted students seeking rigorous academics. Even as the program garnered national attention, however, administrators knew they weren't reaching many students outside the elite program.

With 3,200 students, the high school is one of Maryland's largest, and students outside the magnet program often drifted academically. Today, after nearly a decade of improvement efforts centered on breaking the school up into smaller academies, the school can boast about more than its island of excellence.

The high school has phased in academies in areas including arts and communication, advanced technology, and health and human services. Internships and projects, involving such organizations as the National Institutes of Health, the National Aeronautics and Space Administration, and the Smithsonian Institution bring students and teachers into the workplace.

Academy teachers encourage all students to pursue college-track classes. Ten years ago, 874 students were enrolled in advanced placement (AP) classes in fourteen AP courses. In 2001, 1,635 students were enrolled in seventeen AP classes. Of those who took the AP tests, 72 percent posted passing scores.

"Instead of patting ourselves on our back, we wanted to replicate the success we had in the magnet program for all students," said Laura Grace, the director of academy programs at the school.

Kathy Oliver, who oversees classroom-to-career programs for the Maryland education department, said the programs are an essential element of a strategy to improve academic achievement from kindergarten through graduate school. "This has a lot of momentum in the state," Ms. Oliver said. "It makes learning relevant for students. It answers that question, 'Why am I doing this?'"

CLASSROOM-TO-CAREER CASE STUDIES

Sitka, Alaska: Mt. Edgecombe High School (MEHS)

MEHS offers an unusual example of preparing students for a dynamic global economy because it is Alaska's only public residential school where students come from all over the state and represent many different ethnic groups. Classes reflect the state's close ties to the Pacific Rim, and emphasize the development of entrepreneurial skills.

The vast geography of Alaska demands distance learning, so administrators identified technology as a link with the future of work and learning and invested in equipment and training. Programs were developed to help ensure that students were able to connect to computer networks and to operate sophisticated equipment.

Above all, future success requires the ability to adapt and engage in critical thinking. The program helps students develop self-determination skills by engaging in a process of critical review and evaluation guided by business-derived TQM principles and its own continuous improvement process.

Among its key features are entrepreneurship, critical thinking, technology, Pacific Rim studies, and engaging students and staff in creative ties to the global economy

Phoenix, Arizona: Metro Tech Vocational Institute

Students, about a third of whom have either previously dropped out of school or never attended high school at all, face serious barriers to completing their education. Metro Tech responds with a collection of CTC elements held together by a vision for accomplishing fundamental school reform within a vocational school setting. Elements include curriculum integration, campus-based student enterprises, work-based internships, and technology-based instruction.

The school enjoys a long history of working partnerships with such businesses as Honeywell Commercial Systems Flight Group, AAA of Arizona, Big 4 Restaurants, and Goodwill Industries, each of which has made extraordinary contributions to the school and its students.

Some key program features include academic and vocational integration, technology-based instruction, and campus-based enterprises

East San Gabriel (California) Valley Regional Occupational Program (ESGVROP)

This program serves many minority and poor students in an area threatened by gangs. It represents an outstanding example of an urban school system rising to today's challenges by providing vocational, academic, and support services intended to prepare students to continue their education or obtain employment after high school.

The school cultivates collaborative partnerships with businesses, service agencies, and other educational institutions. Business partners serve on advisory committees, provide labor market data, serve as mentors and job coaches, and provide classrooms for worksite training. Classes are carried out with postsecondary institutions, in some cases through baccalaureate programs. Administrators and staff strive for flexibility in arranging transportation and schedules and providing other support services. An emphasis on research conducted with other educational institutions drives the development of new programs.

Its key features include more than 300 collaborative partnerships with businesses and the community, collaboration with several postsecondary institutions, and reliance on research and program assessment.

Pasadena, California: Graphics Art Academy

Pasadena High School serves a multicultural population whose diversity reflects the changing face of America in the twenty-first century. The academy, a school within a school, serves about 100 students in grades 10–12.

The academy came about from a partnership between the high school and the Printing Industry Association of Southern California, which represents more than 1,900 printing businesses in the greater L.A. area. A five-teacher team integrates the curriculum, combines academic instruction with vocational training, and keeps classes deliberately smaller than regular high school courses to allow cooperative learning and greater student–teacher interaction. Eleventh- and twelfth-grade students take almost all course work within the academy and take advanced courses at Pasadena City College. Its key features use the academy model, integrating academic and vocational classes, and an ongoing partnership with an industry association.

Fort Pierce, Florida: Performance-Based Diploma Program

The program enrolls students from throughout St. Lucie County, Florida, who are considered at risk for dropping out. Also using the school-within-a-school design, the program is a self-paced, mastery-learning program. Students master academics through a computer-assisted instruction (CAI) program.

Instructional leadership is crucial, for although the computer provides the lessons, teachers must be able to quickly help any student in a classroom of thirty, each of whom is in the process of pursuing a different lesson. For vocational study, students choose from traditional high school vocational classes, a dual-enrollment program at the community college, an internship program, or employment at a job they find on their own. All students participate in individual and small-group peer counseling.

The key program features include self-paced mastery learning, the school-within-a-school model, and options for vocational study.

Louisville, Kentucky: Shawnee High School Aviation Magnet

Flying planes, arranging travel reservations, calculating complex flight patterns and time zones, running a cruise ship, and repairing complicated technical equipment—this is all in a day's work for students at Shawnee Aviation Magnet. Within the two strands of aviation and travel/tourism, students actively engage in learning the concepts of their chosen industry, embedded in practical examples and the real-life experience of instructors and students.

In the aviation program, students participate in flight training and can earn an FAA-certified pilot's license or FCC license by the time they graduate. Students in travel and tourism participate in domestic and international internships in which they study and are responsible for all aspects of hotel, travel agency, and cruise operations.

This is a true magnet program with active partnership in major industry areas and local employers with an interdisciplinary curriculum.

Baltimore, Maryland: Baltimore Commonwealth

The Baltimore Commonwealth is an unusual partnership. The city's business, education, community, and government sectors have joined forces to try to improve the prospects of Baltimore high school students for academic achievement, college opportunities, employability, and personal development. The Baltimore Office of Employment Development has created a one-stop shop for student services and for businesses interested in employing students.

Under the Commonwealth umbrella, an array of programs and services is provided, ranging from internships to summer jobs to permanent employment, from career exploration to job readiness skills preparation. There are also Career Clubs for seniors, offered during the high school day, that offer career counseling and coaching to students on specific job-getting and job-keeping skills.

Kalamazoo, Michigan: Valley Consortium Education for Employment Program (EFE)

EFE coordinates a system of occupational education throughout Kalamazoo County, an area including 1.7 million students and nine school districts. The EFE mission is to provide all students with opportunities to obtain basic educational skills, occupational skills, and employability skills. The system consists of more than twenty occupational programs, several work-site-based occupational programs, counseling and information services, and articulation agreements.

There are successful partnerships with major businesses such as the Radisson Hotel and two local hospitals, which have provided facilities for work-site-based occupational programs. A community college is also a full member of the consortium. The system has its own staff: an assistant superintendent, three area administrators, and several vocational counselors and workforce entry coordinators.

The countywide system is based upon a decade of K–14 collaboration, a network of administrators and workforce entry coordinators, and work-site-based occupational programs

Rothsay, Minnesota: Tiger, Inc.

A rural town with a population of 450, harsh winters, and a lagging economy, Rothsay has an innovative high school. It addresses CTC issues and prepares its students for the world of work in creative ways. The strength of Rothsay High School lies in its ability to adapt to challenging economic circumstances and prepare its students to do the same.

Supported by a faculty advisor, students formed a corporation, Tiger, Inc., in 1991. Its first enterprise responded to community need: Tiger, Inc., took over the town's failing grocery store. Students receive credit for staffing the grocery store and the hardware store in capacities such as accounting, advertising, office work, and carpentry. Students also host an entrepreneurial workshop for students and educators from across Minnesota. Teachers attempt to integrate vocational and academic study, teaching specific work skills as well as exploring careers.

Its notable features include student-run enterprises, considerable work experience despite a limited economy, and informal but powerful community ties.

Dayton, Ohio: Patterson Career Center

Started in 1913, Patterson is one of the first cooperative education centers in the nation. Today, it tackles the serious problems confronting urban school systems by striving to offer its students, 82 percent of whom are disadvantaged, a variety of options in an administrative structure that promote participatory management within a broader restructuring process.

Patterson High School works closely with local employers and the community college. It offers eleventh- and twelfth-grade students a schedule that alternates two weeks of classroom instruction with two weeks of full-time, on-the-job work over an eleven-month school year. Teams of academic and vocational instructors hold regularly scheduled cluster meetings several times a week to ensure that academic and vocational components are integrated.

This is an administratively flexible program that alternates academic and work experience tied into continuous learning at the local community college and with local employers.

Eugene, Oregon: Youth Transition Program (YTP)

Policymakers and practitioners across the nation agree that the creation of a seamless classroom-to-career system requires restructuring systems. Oregon is one of the few states that have begun restructuring on a statewide level. YTP is a collaborative effort among the Oregon Department of Education, Oregon Vocational Rehabilitation Division, University of Oregon, and public schools in local communities across the state.

At last count, YTP operates in twenty-six sites across Oregon, helping youth with disabilities make the transition from classroom to career. It aims to provide a new pattern of services to students with disabilities by enhancing the ability of students to enter competitive employment after leaving school and creating systemic change within schools and agencies serving students with disabilities.

It features a statewide program, interagency collaboration, resource redistribution initially focusing on students with disabilities, and wider application for all students; academic and vocational instruction, independent living, and personal/social areas.

Roy, Utah: Roy High School

Students at Roy High School have lots of options as part of a state-level reform effort. Administrators develop flexible schedules for students, resulting in early graduation, innovative use of credits, and communication with postsecondary schools. The core of its innovation lies in its comprehensive counseling and guidance program that finishes in a Student Education and Occupational Plan (SEOP) that is individually crafted for each student.

Planning sessions are held with students and their parents several times a year involving career exploration, self-awareness, career choice, and identifying an appropriate course of study. Students learn more about their options through extensive counseling, a career center with computer accessibility throughout the school, a workplace skills course, and assistance from the local job services agency. Students must meet standards in communication, critical/creative thinking, social and personal development, self-motivation and adaptability, and preparation for life after high school.

Key elements include comprehensive guidance and counseling; individual student plans; expanded day, week, and year courses; and early graduation.

Charlottesville, Virginia: Comprehensive Employment Work and Transition (CEWAT)

CEWAT was created to help students with disabilities find paid job placements and develop good work behaviors, but underwent its own transition and expanded services to at-risk students. Through a partnership between the school and a private nonprofit employment and training agency, the school provides employment specialists who work with students to help them identify job prospects, apply for employment, and negotiate difficulties as they arise after being hired.

A network of employers includes a university dining service, a grocery chain, and nursing home that have hired its students. CEWAT connects students to assessment services provided by the state Rehabilitation Services Administration and to skills training provided by the vocational-technical center. The process of developing Individual Education Plans (IEP) for students with disabilities now includes planning for transition to work.

Veradale, Washington: Student Career Opportunity Paths in Education (SCOPE)

Located a half hour from downtown Spokane, all Veradale students take part in SCOPE, a comprehensive career information and guidance program designed to get students thinking about possible careers before they begin high school. Through inventories of their interests, experiences, and skills, students identify with one of six career paths, each of which contains career options. Students can access both printed and computerized information about the education they would need to pursue a specific career.

Equally important is the infusion throughout the school curriculum of career-related activities, ranging from research assignments to speakers to work experiences. The school hired an experienced local business leader to arrange community placements to provide students with career experience.

Career information, assessment, and guidance systems, career-related activities infused across the curriculum, and a community resource coordinator are key elements.

NOTES

1. Westchester Institute for Human Services Research, 1998.

2. Tennessee Attitudes toward the Workplace, University of Tennessee, Knoxville, 1998.

3. "School-to-Work," *Education Week* (April 11, 2001).

4. School to Work, *Education Week*.

5. Thomas R. Bailey, Katherine L. Hughs, and Melinda J. Mechur, *School to Work: Making a Difference in Education* (New York: Columbia University, February 2001).

6. Richard Kazis and Hillary Pennington, *What's Next for School to Work Career?* (Boston, Mass.: Jobs for the Future, October 1996).

7

CLASSROOM-TO-CAREER
PROGRAMS: BEST PRACTICES

Ninety-six percent of all participants found that a system of education that would provide a strong academic foundation for every student, hands-on learning experiences, and a learning opportunity for
every student to practice what he/she learns in a work-based setting
to be "desirable."[1]
— Education and Workforce Issues, 1997

The local school and the local community need a joint road map to foster mutual commitment to and greater involvement in schools. The
classroom-to-career (CTC) initiatives can be rapidly built around employers who have previously adopted quality improvement programs
such as the Baldrige Education Criteria, ISO 9000-2000, and TQM (total quality management).[2] The connection between CTC initiatives and
quality companies is not just an accident. Part of the initiative to improve process management initiative comes from employers who actively participate in the local community.

SUCCESS STORIES SHOW THE WAY

A major employment sector of the global economy is in the field of information technology (IT). To illustrate the wide-sweeping nature of the

industry, the NSSB catalogue runs sixty-eight pages of different categories for certifications in telecommunications and computer technology.

The following short summary highlights CTC involvement in IT by different types of companies, schools, government bodies, and intermediary organizations and provides samples of partnerships currently underway around the country. It offers fresh thinking, and shows industry participation with other key players in filling the IT skills gap, improving K–16 IT education, and fostering work-based learning experiences for students and teachers.

Autodesk, Inc.

Autodesk, Inc., has a strong corporate commitment to student interns. The world's fourth-largest software company is also a leader in creating IT–CTC initiatives.

Central to this leadership is offering work-based opportunities for students, which include job shadowing, informational interviewing, and internships. Interns become involved in all aspects of Autodesk, from answering a quarter of the Assistance Center's 1,400 calls per week to software testing to working as entry-level employees in the Integrated Media lab.

In 1982, Autodesk was honored by the National Alliance of Business (NAB) with one of their Founders Awards. Since 1992, the company has hosted more than 250 high school and middle school student interns at their corporate headquarters in San Rafael, California.

A recent study by the National Employer Leadership Council found that internships benefit both students and the company. The study shows that CTC participants are achieving at higher academic levels, and Autodesk—one of the companies included in the study—found its financial benefit to be twice its cost.

Capital Area Training Foundation

Austin, Texas, is home to more than 2,500 high-tech companies, including 800 that focus directly on software and IT. Austin is a leader in preparing young people for IT-oriented careers. The Capital Area Training Foundation (CATF), a business-led, nonprofit organization dedicated to building partnerships and relationships between schools and employers, leads the city's classroom-to-career efforts. CATF operates a steering committee in six industry clusters, including hospitality, construction, and high-tech. Its High Tech Committee consists of industry leaders such as Southwest Bell, Motorola, 3M, Pervasive Software, and Time-Warner Cable.

Together with local educators and community leaders, the High Tech Committee helped develop IT courses in several area high schools, created pathways from high school into IT courses at Austin Community College, and organized work-based learning experiences for more than 200 students.

The New York New Media Association

The New York New Media Association (NYNMA), a media trade organization serving the New York metropolitan area, carried out successful internship programs involving thirty-eight students in company-designed, four- to eight-week paid internships, each of which included a specific business-related project.

Company representatives reported on the abilities of the students and their work contributions. Prior to the program, some employers held a stereotypical view of high school-age students. By the end of the first summer, of the thirty-eight students (seventeen high school and twenty-one college) who were placed and hired for paid internship positions at thirty NYC-based new media companies, twenty-two students received job offers to continue their internship into the fall.

The students participating in the NYNMA internships are hired for two kinds of jobs: nontechnical positions (including online research, marketing and public relations, editorial and office administration) and technical internships (such as Web/graphic design, computer programming, technical support, and network administration). All students expressed strong interest in improving their technical skills. Plans are to expand the program to reach over 150 interns drawn from six New York City high schools and four colleges.

Summer programs were funded through the New York State Science and Technology Foundation with New York State Senate Assembly funding. The program was developed and managed for NYNMA by J. Alssid

Associates. The role of an experienced intermediary organization in making this program work was critical.

The program screened and interviewed prospective interns. It recruited companies and set guidelines for their commitment, matched interns and companies, and provided orientations for the educators, students, and company coordinators. The program supported the students throughout the process, including having them keep e-journals focused on key aspects of their experience, and organized speaking programs where the students could learn from entrepreneurs and other professionals. Most important, the program did a thorough job of evaluating all participants (companies, students, etc.).

NYNMA also offered a work-readiness seminar for the high school students involved and recognition ceremony for proper closure at the end of the program.

As expected, companies report different reasons for participating in the NYNMA Internship Program. For some, hiring interns is part of normal operations and the program helped identify new, talented candidates. Other companies signed on because they had an immediate project that they thought would benefit from having intern support. The chance to get needed help at reasonable cost was mentioned by some companies, as was the ability to screen interns as possible future long-term hires.

On the whole, employers report positive experiences and indicate that they would participate again. They noted the interns were crucial to website redesign and a delightful addition to the company overall. Students benefited by developing the soft skills crucial to success at the workplace, sharpening technical skills in a real-world setting, and increasing their awareness of opportunities and realities in a fast-paced IT/new media industry.

The High Technology Council of Maryland

The High Technology Council of Maryland (HTCM), a consortium of more than 600 high-tech companies along with federal labs and government organizations, works with educational institutions to promote high-tech industry in the state. An important part of their mission is both education and workforce development.

The council has been involved in a number of CTC initiatives. There are pilot programs promoting high school and community college internships in IT companies, a program providing educators with the opportunity to visit IT and biotech companies, and paid summer internships for participating educators in high-tech companies.

HTCM cosponsors, along with the Northern Virginia Technology Council and the Greater Washington Board of Trade, an online internship network for college students seeking school year or college internships in the D.C. area. The council recently produced an online student guide (available at www.mdhitech.org/Partners) to resources in high-tech careers.

Greater Louisville, Inc.

Greater Louisville, Inc., part of the Metro Chamber of Commerce, took action in response to IT workforce needs by creating NAME, a coalition of chief information officers (CIO) from thirty local IT companies, to define the skills needed for entry-level information technology employees. An internship system was put together for qualified high school seniors eligible for eight-week internships with member companies.

In the summer of 1999, a pilot class of twenty-two qualified students received internship opportunities and also influenced the secondary schools' curriculum to meet the needs of the employers. For example, the Microsoft certification programs, now an accredited industry standard, are now offered at several local high schools.

Soft Centers

Soft Centers have been up and running in Europe for about fifteen years. Duluth, Minnesota, now also has one thanks to information gained from a Sister Cities tour in Europe. This model is one where businesses and schools colocate in a campuslike setting. Students go to school and intern at the same time with Soft Center companies on projects. Businesses are able to develop, with the college instructors, curriculum that truly fit their industry needs.

The Soft Center Duluth had its grand opening in June 2000 and today provides an impressive array of online resources.[3]

Proctor and Gamble

Proctor and Gamble (P&G) offers co-op and internship positions in IT-related fields, primarily in the management and information systems (MIS) and administrative and technical business areas.

IT intern spots within the P&G business units include programming, software and network infrastructure, systems troubleshooting, and mainframe systems support. P&G management and information systems co-op and internship opportunities include hardware support, software and networking infrastructure; decision support tools; and consulting and operating services to all P&G divisions. A significant number of new P&G IT hires come through the intern and co-op ranks.

The University of Washington

The University of Washington (UW) Information Systems Internship Program has served over 265 students and 100 organizations since its inception in 1999. The Management Science Department at the UW School of Business established the program to provide practical learning experience in professional settings for undergraduate and MBA students concentrating in information systems.

Each student intern works for a sponsoring organization between eight and forty-plus hours per week. All UW interns are paid by the sponsoring organization and students may or may not elect to receive academic credit. If the student elects to receive credit, status reports, meeting attendance, a paper discussing the value of the internship, and a demonstration of knowledge is required.

The experience and exposure gained by the student varies based on the type of business, size of the IT function, and organizational needs. Past interns performed every aspect of work on information systems, recommending and installing hardware, software and networks, and developing systems and training materials. The UW internship program manager works directly with sponsoring organizations to determine requirements, define the scope of and requirements for the internship, and ensure that the sponsoring organization provides educational value to the student.

For entry, students submit their résumés for review by appropriate companies. Then each company interviews at its facilities and selects the student intern. Scheduling and compensation is discussed directly between the company and the student.

The Software Council Fellowship Program

The Software Council Fellowship Program (SCFP), initiated by the Massachusetts Software Council and the commonwealth, provides highly skilled professionals to the commonwealth's huge software industry and helps educate the general public about the unique culture of software companies.

Currently there are four SCFP programs: (1) the fellowship program, for midcareer professionals; (2) the college internship program; (3) software industry overview workshops; and (4) team development retreats.

Modeled after its successful fellowship program, the college internship program provides companies with cost-effective means to meet the demand for entry-level workers. SCFP program staff and company mentors select college seniors and recent graduates for participation in the program. Interns complete a fourteen-week company project, participate in SCFP seminars, develop job readiness skills, and become effective team players.

THE BUILDING BLOCKS OF
CLASSROOM-TO-CAREER INITIATIVES

CTC initiatives benefit students and employers, industries and schools. *The School-to-Work Initiatives: Studies of Education Reform*[4] includes twelve elements, or building blocks, of classroom-to-career systems:

1. Executive leadership
2. Operational leadership
3. Professional development
4. Education leader
5. Cross-sector teamwork
6. Self-determination for all students
7. Transformation of curriculum and instructional practice
8. Work-based learning strategies

9. Career counseling in the system
10. Communication with postsecondary institutions
11. Seed money for CTC reform
12. Applications research

It always starts from the top. CTC needs an advocate at the executive level to increase the likelihood that the reform takes root throughout the educational system. CTC is likely to remain a fragmented activity unless it has *executive leadership*.

Successful transition systems demand leaders who can develop a shared vision, clear goals, and a comprehensive strategy, and enlist the support and involvement of all stakeholders. Beyond vision and advocacy, these leaders operate with a keen sense of politics, both in understanding the process and in knowing the players. They are willing to take risks and recognize that change demands time, mistakes, and a tolerance of failure.

The CTC program deliverer provides *operational leadership* covering a wide variety of roles: instructors, counselors, transition specialists, CTC coordinators, and others. Some delivery roles belong to certain positions—instructors provide classroom training, for example—but other roles, such as communication with business partners, may be delegated or shared in various ways. As leaders, program deliverers must possess excellent organizational and communication skills. As reformers, they must have a deep knowledge of education, curriculum, the industry, and the student population.

Whether their training is academic or experiential, effective program deliverers also understand youth development and learning theory, including the variety of learning styles and the stages of adolescent development. Effective program deliverers have some understanding, usually earned through actual industry experience, of the occupational area within which the CTC program provides training.

For a reform effort to successfully take root in a local school system, classroom practices, counseling sessions, and administrative processes must change. *Professional development* is one route that CTC initiatives adopt in order to engage school staff in the reform, ensuring that at least some staff will change their professional practices sufficiently to support the vision and strategies of the reform.

The *education leader* makes professional development a priority for that school, district, or regional entity. Like so many aspects of CTC, professional development may conflict with standard school schedules and logistics, which can block the effort unless an administrator in a position of some authority runs interference and clears the way.

A CTC transition system is by definition dependent on effective *cross-sector teamwork* among all of the education stakeholders. The first step in developing a representative system is taking stock of the range of partners in a community. Partners must be engaged early in the process to foster a sense of empowerment and ability to influence the shape of the system. Effective long-term teamwork requires broad and inclusive recruitment and continuous nurturing of partnerships so that all the partners recognize the rewards, risks, and long-term outcomes they can expect for the students and themselves.

Different partners call for different types of reassurances that the CTC system can work for them. The goal of such extensive and carefully nurtured partnerships comes about in an atmosphere of shared vision, beliefs, and resources.

In order to help students prepare for a lifetime of learning, fulfilling work, and productive adult lives, CTC transition systems must support the development of *self-determination for all students*.

Students need to be encouraged to take responsibility for their learning, to manage their career options, and to develop social skills and a maturity level that will help them interact positively with adults and peers. This is especially true for at-risk students, because the school system may be the only vehicle for them to learn how to cope with the complexities of adult life.

At the heart of CTC reform is a *transformation of curriculum and instructional practice* so that learning is contextual (i.e., learning that occurs in a real-life situation, or as a close simulation of a real-life circumstance). Curriculum and instruction in such a transition system provides multiple connection points between the work and learning experiences. The successful CTC curriculum links demanding academic study with up-to-date vocational instruction and work-readiness preparation.

Whatever the classroom curriculum, it must connect in a rational and supportive way to the workplace learning experience. The measurement of learning that takes place in such settings is so unlike the traditional classroom that it requires correspondingly different assessment practices. CTC programs draw up comprehensive sets of competencies, often in consultation with business partners, to test students in the program.

Some establish comprehensive standards toward which all the programs within a school or district are expected to strive. Others experiment with portfolio assessment as the most accurate way to document a student's education.

Successful transition systems offer a variety of *work-based learning strategies* and experiences that build on local labor market conditions and allow for differences in student interests, aptitudes, and developmental stages. Transition systems can include a menu of options such as business-based experiences, school-based enterprises, entrepreneurial programs, youth apprenticeships, mentorship, cooperative education, and service learning.

Programs also apply a range of strategies, paid or unpaid work during the school day or after school, or based in a school or community classroom. Programs are customized to fit the needs of youths, schools, businesses, and the local community. Regardless of which particular options or strategies a CTC system uses, it must provide logistical support to students, staff, and business partners.

A critical component for effective CTC transition systems is tying *career counseling into the system*. In addition to career information, assessment, and guidance, many programs provide mentoring and personal counseling activities. These services are not appendages but essential elements of the system.

Such services must be ongoing, and each student needs an individual education and career plan that is regularly updated. CTC counseling must link into earlier grades and age-appropriate activities that start in elementary school. There are multiple points at which counseling needs to occur, and it must be ongoing and consistently available to students. Most important, the school counseling system must tie into reliable, up-to-date labor market and job information sources.

Programs that do not start until eleventh grade miss the chance to make a difference for many students. It is increasingly crucial to reach younger students—before the eleventh grade—before they become discouraged, disengaged, or drop out. Common sense and sound research support the fact that a student who understands the link between school and work—between lifelong learning and a successful life—will be much more motivated to succeed in school and have a jump start on life.

Communication with postsecondary institutions while the student is still in high school may take the form of dual/concurrent enrollment, college credit for high school courses, the acceptance by postsecondary institutions of alternative forms of assessment such as portfolios or certificates of mastery, or an agreement that the postsecondary institution will grant credit for alternative instruction such as work-based learning experiences.

Such arrangements greatly expand the training immediately available to high school students, and offer them a ladder of opportunity toward progressively more advanced training and advantageous employment after high school.

Just as an effective CTC system begins before eleventh grade, it extends beyond high school graduation. Programs must provide multiple connections to postsecondary institutions, beginning when the student is still in high school and extending to provide post–high school education and training options.

In its early stages, *seed money for CTC reform* is always a critical element of these initiatives. Many initiatives have drawn on federal funding, including Perkins Act and other vocational and special populations grants. Where the state government has supported tech prep and related reforms, state funds have made a significant difference. In some states, funds for educational reform, including specific set-asides for CTC transition, have helped schools initiate such reforms.

Businesses too have provided funds, in-kind contributions, and human resources that have not only underwritten specific programs but also offered evidence of corporate support that helps leverage more support. Interagency agreements that allow education programs to draw on other governmental funds, particularly those set aside for employment and training or for special populations, greatly benefit CTC transition systems in several states.

A number of the CTC programs have conducted their own *applications research* or commissioned new research in order to better plan, assess, or strengthen their CTC system. They've made use of research to provide a foundation for a program model; to assess the local labor market and economy; and to measure the impact of the program on students, specifically how their graduates fared in the worlds of work and postsecondary education.

Using research also brings a number of secondary benefits. The findings help demonstrate justification for the CTC system, affirm to staff the importance of their work, leverage additional resources for support, and provide feedback to learn from mistakes—to improve and refine aspects of the reform initiative.

THE LOCAL SCHOOL STARTS GOOD PRACTICES EARLY

In 1998, the author conducted a study of ongoing school quality initiatives in selected states under a grant from the Florida Department of Education. One of the states visited was New Mexico, where we learned firsthand how the New Mexico SQS (Strengthening Quality Schools) program was progressing.

Quality is a statewide obsession in New Mexico, and not just in its schools. In Albuquerque we visited Mrs. Edwards and her first-grade class at the Georgia O'Keeffe Elementary School. As soon as we entered the classroom, we noticed a prominently posted list of TQM (total quality management) standards to which class members had agreed to subscribe. At the time, these first graders were actively involved in building their own website.

In preparing this update, I electronically visited Mrs. Edwards' first-grade class.[5] Here are the posted 2002 standards:

Our Vision . . . to Be a TQ Team!

---

1. We care about each other.

2. Our teacher is happy, proud, and loves us.

3. We come to school ready to learn.

4. We trust ourselves.

5. We make good decisions.

6. We don't say, "I can't."

7. We learn from our mistakes.

8. We solve our problems ourselves.

9. We make good choices.

10. We don't tattle unless it's appropriate.

11. We're serious about meeting our goals.

12. We have fun and laugh a lot.

13. We keep on trying . . . persevere.

14. We are the best that we can be.

15. We're not perfect, but we're always improving.

16. We make our teachers happy.

WHAT SCHOOLS NEED FROM BUSINESS PARTNERS

From time to time, all of us yield to fads and fashions. Businesses, however, can offer the local school something that no one else can offer—staying power on the issue of education improvement. Local companies and businesses have an ongoing presence and investment in the community that is not found elsewhere.

The business community can help bring to the local school and district an expanded vision. Many business leaders see the public school system in its historic context of once having been out front but in recent years falling behind. It is hard to disagree with them.

For too long now, the local school has carried the remnants of assembly-line process thinking: put children in one end when they're five years old and discharge them out the other end when they're eighteen. At this point, these "cogs" are supposed to be close to a finished product—but this simply does not work anymore, if in fact it ever did.

Businesses need to ask the local school system, "Why don't you give us a concept of something else?" The largest institution in America is the public schools. Is it realistic to expect school leaders to be visionary after decades of tradition?

As a rule, there are always a few good principals, a few good superintendents, and lots of good teachers—but the kind of vision needed is not likely to come from within the institution. The vision needs to come from outside. Here is where the business community can really provide much help.

Business leaders need to figure out how to get inside an institution that deep down really doesn't want them in there. How many business leaders are invited in to help the schools, other than financially? For that matter, how many business leaders have even asked to be let in? As a rule, the business leader feels let off the hook if he gives money to the schools and then takes a hike. It is here where CTC and the use of such performance management processes, such as ISO 9000 and the Baldrige, intersect.

The Industrial Age view of transforming students was one of transforming workers into raw material and using workers as a component tool of production-line manufacturing. One can picture Charlie Chaplin straining to turn nuts and bolts on a speeded-up production line in the movie *Modern Times,* or Lucille Ball packing chocolates on a speeded-up conveyor belt on her TV show. Contrast this with the twenty-first-century production and service entity that increasingly uses information technology to bring its workers along to meet changing industry quality standards and rising international competitive standards.

Businesses cannot really help their local communities to any great degree unless they are certain they understand the political environment that surrounds education. It is relatively easy for a business to send its lobbyist to the state legislature or to Congress when it is a bottom-line issue for a company. If the company is going to be disadvantaged by, say, proposed legislation dealing with clean air, it knows right where to go in that legislative process to make sure the company is not put at a disadvantage. The same holds true if it is a transportation issue. Businesses know exactly where to go in the proposed legislation in order to fix it.

However, local schooling is not quite that straightforward. First, it's not too easy to pinpoint a place that needs to be fixed to make the local school perform better, especially in a fast-changing and increasingly uncertain global economy. Business leaders need to take the time to think through the process of trying to understand the school system itself, and that is tough and time consuming. It wears people down.

Another barrier is the strange language of education that is actually the culture of the field. Take the jargon of educators, for example. As one story goes, while attending a meeting on higher education, a person holding a Ph.D. in education speaks to a business group. She uses the phrase "culminating experience."

The businesspersons, meanwhile, sit around the table looking mystified. Finally, she is asked by another educator: "Doctor, I think I may have had two of those culminating experiences in my time, but exactly what are you talking about?"

Drawing on her master's thesis followed by a summary of her doctoral dissertation, the education Ph.D. answers and the questioner replies, "Yes, I have had two of those culminating experiences."

The group of businesspeople who came away from this exchange hadn't the foggiest notion of what a "culminating experience" was. I'm not sure I know what a culminating experience is.[6] Yet the phrase is bandied about by educators confident that their audiences will understand them.

If business leaders are going to be successfully involved in local education, they must learn to appreciate its language and its traditions while helping educators join the mainstream.

Another thing that shocks businesspeople is the budgeting process in education. In traditional public school systems, cutbacks are out of the question. Have you ever seen an educational program dissolved because it didn't work?

From my own experience as a school board president, I recall the time when in frustration I blurted out to the district chief financial officer, "We sure wouldn't do it that way in my company," to which he immediately shot back, "This isn't your company." I thought then and there, just because it's a school district doesn't mean it shouldn't be run in a businesslike manner.

Look around the educational community and ask yourself this: "Where are the points of resistance to change?"

Don't be surprised where you find them. They are on the school board, with the parents, among the teachers, some of the administrators, buried in the legislature, and widespread among voters. In every local community, businesses must set about to help build new coalitions with disparate groups. And if businesses do not talk to them, there is an automatic no.

The most resistant group is the local school board. The next most resistant group is the state legislature. Forget the hyperbole; neither
group's members are particularly in a hurry to break with tradition.

FROM HIGH TECH TO HIGH TOUCH

Southwest Florida has a wealth of resorts, hotels, and golf courses but is
in increasingly short supply of people qualified to run the resorts that
draw thousands of tourists to that area each year. Finally, resort industry
leaders took the bull by the horns.

In mid-2002, industry leaders and educators started working jointly to
raise more than $10 million to start a bachelor's program in resort and
hospitality management at Florida Gulf Coast University (FGCU), part
of the state university system, located in Ft. Myers (Lee County),
Florida.[7] One hope is that if students come to southwest Florida for
their studies, they will decide to stay there. In a global economy and
transient age, that goal may prove more elusive than doable.

Southwest Florida is a land of resorts, so such a new college program
would seem to be a natural fit. But in the wake of September 11, all state
university campuses face budget cuts. This means chopping programs
rather than adding.

The university lacks the money to fund a start-up hospitality management program, but many hospitality industry leaders (especially those in
four- and five-star resorts located in Naples) recognized the need and
began lobbying the university for such a program.

The result: People in the local hospitality industry agreed to help raise
money to pay for the university program's first four years. After that, the
program is expected to be self-sufficient.

Tourism is "high touch," though there are many "high-tech" elements
in the marketing and service centers. About 36,000 people in Lee
County work in tourism, including hotels, attractions, and restaurants,
making it the region's number one employer, and tourism brought an estimated $1.7 billion into the area in 2001. But the industry needs to re-
cruit managers and more workers from outside the area. The complaint
is that there are no "home-grown" managers.

If the university can raise $1.4 million to pay for a director, three faculty members, and staff by January 2003, the program could start in the fall of 2003.

FGCU has a pretty good handle on the kind of program it wants but "all" the university has to do is come up with the money. Administrators have also proposed plans for an $8.4-million building for the program.

If the school raises half of that amount, the state will match the rest. The FGCU program would focus on resort management rather than just hotel management. Resorts are more than filling and cleaning hotel rooms. Resorts offer leisure activities such as golf and tennis, and cater to the recreational wants of vacationers rather than the overnight and meeting needs of business travelers.

This is a different side of the hospitality industry and it takes different training. The program would also offer a specialty in golf course management because the area has a wealth of golf pros needing good staff. Administrators plan to use the PGA Professional Golf Management program, which trains students to become club professionals.

The region's golf courses and resorts offer plenty of opportunity for internships and classroom-to-career experiences. Florida, with its beaches, golf courses, cruise lines, hotels, and resorts, seems to be an obvious place to study hospitality management.

The Institute for Hospitality and Tourism Education and Research at Florida International University (FIU), located in the Miami-Dade area, has a nationally recognized hospitality management program. It recently launched a distance-learning program that allows students to earn a master's degree in twenty months.

The core of the classroom-to-career message is that a good classroom-to-career program caters to *local* employment needs. It depends on what the industry is looking for; in Southwest Florida, they look to start people in middle management. There's a need for all types of managers. There is also a great need for competent and customer-centered resort staff. In southwest Florida school districts serving heavy resort areas in Collier, Lee, and Sarasota Counties, there are ample opportunities for CTC programs starting in the secondary school.

Year after year, there isn't a resort manager in Collier or Lee Counties that can look you in the eye and say that he doesn't have a fear when the season starts. Finding and keeping the right people is a challenge.

TURNING THE TIDE

Surprisingly, one of the least resistant groups to using CTC are the teachers. Teachers are willing to change and try new approaches if they can be somewhat deregulated. If we say to a teacher, "Do it this way for eight hours a day," we get resistance; if we say to a teacher, "How would you like to be free to create a better educational environment in your classroom, and we will even pay you a little money if you've got a good idea?" we can get a lot of support.

Teachers and students need to be shown that education leaders and stakeholders care how well they are doing. Too many students, because of myriad causes, have the feeling that no one cares.

Schools were not meant to build the self-esteem of young people. Unfortunately, the level of esteem held by most of young people is such that the schools have to take this on. It seems that when we can't fix a problem at home and we can't fix it in the community, we assign it to the schools to fix. Right now, schools carry a heavier load than they can handle.

Schools can help increase student self-esteem by recruiting mentors for each student. Because it is all volunteer labor, setting up a mentoring program takes only a small amount of money. In place of money, however, mentoring takes strong commitment. The business community is increasingly helpful in setting up mentoring programs.

We need to reward educational entrepreneurs. One proponent of merit pay proposes good teachers be paid fantastically well and poor teachers penalized financially. But try to get a merit pay system into a school or school district and watch carefully where the challenges come from. And really, which of us would want our children schooled by a poor teacher who is also penalized financially?

We must find ways to encourage educational entrepreneurs. Somehow, we have to develop an educational system that lets educators take risks and rewards them for doing so. Why should we assume that our educational system should be risk free?

There are risks in education just like there are risks in business, in war, and in government and politics.

"Blessed are they who expect very little for they shall not be disappointed," goes the old saying. For too long now we have expected too little in the way of quality student performance from our schools. Now, we must take more risks to advance the cause of higher expectations for our schools, for the students, for the parents, and for all stakeholders. But we cannot mandate results.

THE VISION OF SUCCESS

The power of "voluntary standards" is demonstrated in the more than 100-year experience of the Underwriters Laboratories (UL). The history of UL tracks closely the development of electrical products in the United States.

UL was the first to develop a safety standard for colored Christmas lights. It was UL that spread the first building safety standards after the great San Francisco fire of 1905. To this day, the UL label remains a voluntary requirement not enforced by any government. But in order to sell a product, especially a product having safety considerations such as electrical or fire hazard, the product must carry the UL label or risk being rejected by the customer.

During the earlier-mentioned field survey of quality school systems, we visited Joseph Sabatella, regional superintendent of schools in Woodbury, Connecticut, who had been honored with the Connecticut Quality Award. Talking about public education, Sabatella said: "If evolution of the species were dependent on change in the public school system, I am convinced we would have the opportunity today to visit a real Jurassic Park."

More and more we hear these three words—what's the use? These come from educators and employers alike who are disappointed with the work-readiness of students. Schools are pressed to improve results while parents thrash about for new solutions and grab on to vouchers, charter schools, or any alternative to public schools—including home schooling.

The American worker and American workplace face a fiercely competitive free-market global economy. It is a new world of economic necessity driven by knowledge workers. But American workers increasingly face serious gaps when competing with the rest of the developed nations.

U.S. employers report local schools continue to lose ground. A survey of more than 4,000 members of the National Association of Manufacturers (NAM) reported employer costs for remedial training jumped from .5 percent of payroll costs in 1991 to 2 percent of payroll costs in 1996; that translates to $11.5 billion spent reworking the output of our schools![8]

Employers ranked labor quality up there along with regulatory problems as their number one important problem. A decade ago, labor quality ranked only sixth on the list of small business concerns.

For years now, educators have been steadily pummeled with "y'oughtas." You ought to do this! You ought to do that! Millions of pages on improving education have been bound into thousands of books and reports that today line miles of bookshelves. The relentless focus on "educational input" (or commonly called "more money") has had a counterintuitive effect on "educational results." The customers of education deserve an approach that works.

We have reached the apex of thirty years of work to present achieving results in schools through quality control and accountability. In "Teaching Tactics," the delivery of quality education and accountability, as one would run a business, is explored.[9] Since its publication, American business has drilled deeper into its arsenal of management principles to discover CTC initiatives supported by total quality management is the tool to help gain a new edge.[10]

USING MEASURES THAT WORK

For too many years, schools have failed to measure the full costs of delivering a workforce-ready student to the graduation stage. From an accountability standpoint, continuing to measure only the cost-per-student taught (input) and not the cost-per-student-learned (output) remains a major blunder: What is taught and what is learned are not the same thing.

We are not including the cost of nonoperable units—by that we mean students, graduates, or dropouts who are functionally illiterate or who cannot perform in today's workplace and society. The public schools duck this issue of arriving at a full cost of delivering a ready-to-work student.

Continuing to rely upon the "input" measurement is apparent in recent lawsuits in New Jersey. To address the funding problems of urban districts, the New Jersey Supreme Court ruled that the state aid formula must enable twenty-eight special-needs urban districts to spend as much per child as is spent in the state's most affluent districts. Not to be outdone, a group of mostly rural school districts filed a lawsuit charging that the governor's school-funding plan does not give them enough money to provide the "thorough and efficient" education required by the state constitution. Irrespective of urban poor, affluent suburban, or mixed rural district, the one thing that employers generally agree upon is that they want and need results.

Developing knowledge skills is the business of schools. Parents want their kid prepared (output) to gain his or her share of the American dream (a good job and quality of life). Employers want a work-ready employee (one who can be given responsibilities and has thinking and judgment skills). In the free-market global economy, the American dream rides on knowledge skills.

Workforce development is a major concern and employers increasingly look to CTC programs to help increase the number of "operable units" ready for work. Why should an American employer settle for a less-than-prepared American worker when he or she can go almost anywhere in the world and find better-schooled workers with greater personal initiative at lower cost?

USING REFRIGERATOR-DOOR LANGUAGE

Americans see themselves as quick learners in a fast-paced world, so let's try keeping CTC simple.

Start by demonstrating a vision to displace the fear of change and build long-term acceptance of continuous improvement in the local school and local community. The leading CTC initiatives build on four key findings:

1. Show results quickly; recognizing team objectives early builds confidence.
2. Next, consolidate early breakthroughs by applying a school-based CTC program.

3. Link CTC to new workplace standards to assure twenty-first-century readiness.

4. Certify results by CTC matching acknowledged industry standards.

The basic principles to promote effective decision making and problem solving, the vision, and proposed structure of improved CTC initiatives and results are here.

Since things are never simple, first look for and then understand the hidden linkages—the interconnected parts that flow directly from the power of a team effort.

NOTES

1. Education and Workforce Issues: Public Attitudes and Awareness, Elway Research, Inc., Davis Tietse and Co., 1997.

2. Allen Salowe and Leon Lessinger, *Healing Public Schools: Curing Their Chronic Illness* (Lanham, Md.: Scarecrow Education Press, 2001) presents an in-depth discussion of quality principles in school improvement. For further information specific to ISO 9000-2000, see www.iso-9000-2000.com.

3. Soft Center Duluth can be reached at www.softcenterduluth.org.

4. *School-to-Work Initiatives: Studies of Education Reform* (Washington, D.C.: US DoE Office of Educational Research, October 1996). Available at www.ed.gov/pubs/SER/SchoolWork/.

5. "Mrs. Edwards' First-Grade Class," Georgia O'Keeffe Elementary School Albuquerque, New Mexico, at www.okeeffe.aps.edu.

6. For the curious, California Polytechnic State University defines "culminating experience" as "the successful completion of a thesis, project, or comprehensive examination for the granting of a graduate degree."

7. Alison Gerber, *The Ft. Myers News-Press* (May 17, 2002).

8. A *Wall Street Journal* survey of 699 small businesses (December 16, 1997).

9. "Teaching Tactics," *Wall Street Journal* (May 30, 1978).

10. See Salowe and Lessinger, *Healing Public Schools*.

8

FOCUSING ON OUR TIME

Here's a message to post on the bulletin board of every school in America:

> *The requirements for earning a decent living and achieving a quality of life in twenty-first-century America are not the same as they were in the past. See your teachers for details.*

THE UNAVOIDABLE LINK OF OUR TIME

Time and again, we stress the inevitable link between a well-paying career and a quality education. We are not just talking about professional work and years of college, though the facts bear this out. We are also talking about any well-paying mainstream job in a knowledge economy and how it links to the quality of K–12 schooling, or however far one travels in his or her continuous learning.

There are few connections that are so clear, so direct, and so dramatic. The more we learn and the better we learn it, the more we can

earn and the greater our satisfaction with our work and the economic dimension of our life.

EASIER SAID THAN DONE

On April 14 and 15, 2002, the *Palm Beach Post* published a series of
frank and disturbing stories dealing with student discipline in the Palm
Beach County, Florida, schools.[1] Until now, this area had been known
for sun and fun, vacation homes of the rich and famous, and the "hang-
ing chads" of the 2000 presidential election.

The disturbing truth is that many of the reported discipline-problem
stories came as no surprise to teachers, administrators, and parents of
school-age kids. Disruptive student behavior has ranged from assaulting
teachers to tearing up the classroom to writing obscene messages on the
walls. Students repeatedly curse teachers and call them unprintable names
when they do not feel like doing assignments or following directions.

After a while, the teacher says nothing for fear of what the kids will
do. In Texas, a study showed 65 percent of teachers were intimidated
from taking action to quell student behavior by the threat of a potential
lawsuit. This insidious form of terrorism is right under our nose in the
public school classroom and we either choose not to see it or are help-
less to do something about it.

Even honor students are increasingly coming to class with "attitude."
Should this attitude problem come as any surprise? Look at consumer
advertising for a moment. Pontiac boasts its new cars have attitude
while Abercrombie and Fitch promotes youth-market image clothing
adorned with art that bespeaks attitude, and parents display an outrageous auto bumper sticker that proudly boasts "My kid can beat up
your honor student."

We are surrounded by TV opinion shows that pit two sides of the issue into a contest of how much attitude can be displayed to overshout
informed opinion. Movies feature the display of attitude as the central
heroic theme in "the end justifies the means" drama. And let's not over-
look the Little League parents who allow attitude to overcome good
judgment to the point of vicious assault or, in one case, manslaughter.
And we can't forget the Lake Worth, Florida, middle school student who

let attitude overpower his better sense when he left the school, went home and got a gun, returned to school, threatened his "favorite" teacher, and then shot him dead.

This stuff is no longer humorous, if in fact it ever was intended to be. And "constitutional right" is not an explanation for the just plain bad taste and poor judgment that affect the growing up of every school-age child.

IDLENESS BREEDS TROUBLE

Teachers report repeated accounts of chaotic classrooms where smart-aleck students make a habit of disobedience—stealing teachers' attention and disrupting learning for the rest of the children.

Student discipline problems are the worst teachers have ever seen, and school records bear this out. For 2000–2001, unruly student behavior in Palm Beach County rose districtwide to over 200,000 incidents, up 5 percent from the previous year.[2] The number of students with disciplinary infractions reportedly had also risen sharply among middle schoolers. Teachers describe administrators as brushing aside behavior problems for fear of a negative image or they're simply overwhelmed with other duties; parents provide little support.

At Roosevelt Middle School (where our daughter teaches environmental science and our granddaughter attends seventh grade), a student spit in a teacher's coffee.[3] The personal stories we are told sound like exaggerations until we realize she is living this nightmare. At West Riviera Elementary, a Florida F-grade school, two girls got into a fight so nasty that one smashed a coffee pot to use the sharp edges as a weapon. Students have thrown desks at teachers and threatened to have them beaten up.[4]

Student behavior is the school's number one problem and it's getting worse. Many teachers leave the profession after hitting a retirement threshold but most are driven out by the frustration of constantly reprimanding students and seeing the classroom control tactics fizzle amid students who are "deceitful."

One teacher describes it like dog biscuit training. If students don't see the teacher holding the biscuit, they won't do the right thing just because it's the right thing to do. It's tough to teach and have students learn when a comparatively small number of kids wreak large amounts of havoc on the classroom.

A thirty-year veteran English teacher in Palm Beach County reported that he found it easier when he switched to one of the county's alternative schools set up for repeat discipline problems. The classroom size dropped to about fifteen students from the normal thirty-student classroom. The teaching is more tolerable in the alternative school because it is stricter and manages student time more tightly. This cuts down on discipline problems.

THREE DS AND THE THREE RS

School officials around the country attribute growing student behavioral problems to a variety of factors. First among these, administrators are fearful of being sued for disciplining too harshly, as uncovered in the Texas report. Unruly kids figure this out real fast. Principals are afraid of having the "bad school" label placed on their building and therefore set aside teacher concerns. Students can take further advantage of this admittedly "gun-shy" administrative mind-set.

Most disturbing, there has been a marked shift in societal thinking that left educators at the bottom of the totem pole in the eyes of parents and students. Kids are the first to step into and take advantage of this gap. And there is always the ever-present broken family run by dysfunctional parents or relatives who are not effective in raising children.

Teachers are given classroom assignments today where students are no longer either ready or willing to learn. Teachers get students who come to class already lagging behind their peers academically, coming from unstable homes, or with survival concerns more pressing than school agendas. So the kids are frustrated and act out in school. More than low salaries or concern for school violence, discipline problems get the teacher's attention. This is what eventually beats down the teachers and prompts many of them to quit the profession.

"The bulk of the problems in our classrooms are the three D's: disruptive behavior, disorderly conduct, disrespectful language," said Alison Adler, director of the Palm Beach County District's Safe Schools Center. "In the old days, when I was in school, teachers got classrooms where students were ready and willing to learn."

Discipline is an especially knotty problem in middle schools, according to an analysis of school district figures, based on incidents reported by school administrators. Students in the district's middle schools in 2001 committed almost 109,000 incidents, from stealing and pulling a false fire alarm to cheating and battery. That averages three incidents for every middle school student.[5] Two-thirds of those incidents—almost 76,000—were discipline problems affecting the classroom: disruptive behavior, disobedience and insubordination, rules violations, and disrespectful language. This marked a 13 percent increase from the 1999–2000 year.

The numbers are not as high in the elementary and high schools, where reported incidents actually decreased. But students in grades K–6 and 9–12 still have the same tendencies toward the "three Ds" as middle schoolers.

Students who repeatedly misbehave in class carry a hefty price tag for taxpayers.

If the students are placed in an alternative education program, the annual individual cost to educate them jumps by 50 percent or greater.

TEACHERS SET THE TONE

Like it or not, accept it or not, education experts say the teacher sets the tone of the classroom from the first day. Yet in most teacher's colleges and universities, courses in classroom management are not even required for a teaching certificate. Fighting back, teachers insist student behavior shouldn't be all their responsibility. They ask, "Where are the parents?"

"You simply can't put this all on teachers," said University of Virginia professor Robert Pianta, who specializes in classroom management and student behavior. "Sometimes the problem lies in the parents, who can be as ill-behaved as the students," Pianta said.

Problems vary from school to school and classroom to classroom. Every year it's something new. Most teachers work on the assumption that behavior management is one of those things where you just have to try different things and see what works.

It's like some of the problems reported in the U.S. military. Today's raw recruit is less schooled, enlists with an "attitude," and is tougher to

mold into a real soldier. Should the drill sergeant blame it on the recruit's parents? Or just learn how to break in a new recruit as one would
break and train an unruly horse?

A SINGLE SET OF RULES

Follow the action. Just before the 8:30 bell, the Crestwood Middle
School principal picks up her hand-held radio and says, "Time to fly, Ea-
gles." Then, she speed-walks, followed by her secretary and other office
employees to their sentry points.

This is Crestwood, and no matter the reason, late is late.[6]

The second bell rings, signaling the start of the next period, and a
nervous sixth-grader is caught on the first step leading to his class.
"You're tardy," says a teacher.

Principal Vera Garcia knows how much work went into that teacher's
words. It took about a half-day of staff debate, but this is what tardy
means at Crestwood: You are not inside the classroom when the second
bell rings. Every teacher has agreed on this definition, and every teacher
enforces it. The school is not a courtroom for hearing an ongoing debate.

"We're all speaking the same language," Garcia says.

More and more, Palm Beach County schools are beginning to speak
this language, as teachers struggle with escalating levels of student mis-
behavior that chews up classroom time and creates a general atmosphere of chaos.

Called "single-school culture," the discipline system has attracted national attention from publications such as *Education Week* and has kept
its creator, Alison Adler, busy. She has helped at least seven county
schools implement the system. What does a single-school culture mean?
Simply this, the definition of culture is the phrase "The way we do things
around here."

Single-school discipline means that in every classroom, the rules and
the punishments are the same. There are no excuses, no varying "inter-
pretations" of a rule. The hall pass requirement is firm, and the consequences do not depend on a teacher's whim or how persuasive or assertive is the student.

In a previous book, we have written that teachers think, "When that door shuts it's my classroom and my rules."[7] So then the teacher believes his or her rules circumvent the school rules. This brings chaos. When students do not see a consistent discipline across the school, they perceive it as uneven and unfair.

This is one of the inconsistencies that drive high teacher turnover, estranged kids, staff tension, poor academic results, and even more intense student behavior.

The single-school culture serves to even things out. It makes kids much less likely to go against the grain. It levels the playing field with a consistent set of ground rules

Garcia sums it up: "Be fair, be consistent, and keep letting them know the rules. It's not magic, but it's effective."[8]At Christa McAuliffe Middle School, named for the first teacher lost in the *Challenger* space tragedy, teachers and administrators on the school discipline committee got fed up repeatedly talking about the same problems.

Too many tardy students wasted class time as the teacher debated whether the student's foot was in the door when the bell rang. Youngsters wander the halls with a "pass" made out of torn paper from a teacher's desk. Students roam the campus without an I.D. badge. Finally they decided, why are we still talking about this, let's do something about it.

Adler came in and embarked on the same process pioneered three years earlier. The entire Christa McAuliffe staff, from teachers to secretaries to the school police officer, sat down to create a detailed policy for hall passes.

They came up with a can't-miss-it neon pink sheet, carried on a clipboard and marked with the teacher's initials, that details the student carrier's name and when they are expected at their destination. An unannounced tour of Christa McAuliffe hallways found all students carrying the bright forms and heading to their destinations with the speed of determined holiday shoppers.

This is the kind of action that ripples out to affect everything else in the system. As students go from class to class, they know exactly what is expected and it feeds back through a continuous loop to impact the whole school.

A single-school culture does not just ease discipline problems. It allows students and teachers to spend more time on math and English when they are not busy testing each other's limits. And teachers who are able to actually teach—rather than spend half the class writing detentions—are also more likely to stick around.

THE APPLE DOESN'T FALL FAR FROM THE TREE

Consequences are an essential element to improving student academic achievement and the quality of life in the local school. Meeting simple but consistent rules is its own reward.

Only about one in ten Americans say it is very common to encounter children or teenagers who treat others with respect.[9] Less than a third of public high school students report their classmates typically treat their teachers or others with respect.[10]

When Vera Garcia introduces herself to parents at the start of the school year, she warns them that if children break the rules at her school, there will be consequences. The parents usually cheer, applaud, and whistle. They're all in favor of the rules—until their child breaks them.[11]

This is an increasingly common theme at schools around the country as education leaders work to take back control of their classrooms. What happened to the parents? Many teachers, principals, counselors, and administrators grieve over the once-supportive role of parents that has now become increasingly absent or even combative.

We can hear it in the language used by students today. "My mom doesn't care," says a typical seventh-grader flatly, "because she talks the same way."

But it is crucial for teachers and administrators to have parents on their side. The local school needs the parent as a partner. Teachers can do their best to enforce rules and behavior plans, but children spend only about seven hours a day in the classroom. Good behavior needs to be reinforced at home.

Most teachers and principals remember when things were different. They fondly recall when parents almost never argued with teachers, let alone screamed at them. They can't pinpoint when it all changed, but it seems most parents today aren't the same as parents twenty years ago, many educators say.

"I think every principal has had the experience where a child gets into trouble, we call the parents, and then they just come in and yell and scream at us," says Christa McAuliffe principal Terry Costa. "I can't imagine my parents ever doing that. I think it's a whole societal issue. If parents aren't instilling respect for authority, how can we get kids to respect it?"

The school social worker lays the blame for this mess on the disintegration of the traditional family and overworked parents causing much of today's classroom discipline problems. The erosion of the family is a big problem with both parents working and not getting get home until late at night. Maybe it's just a mother raising the child on her own. Kids are acting out of anger because the parents aren't there.

But it is also not realistic for schools to lay all the responsibility at the feet of parents, especially in an age where single-parent families are as common as traditional families. Across the nation, single moms outnumber two-parent households for the first time ever, according to 2000 census numbers.

But none of these family demographics excuse too many parents failing to teach respect to their kids. "The apple doesn't fall far from the tree. I can see why children behave a certain way when I meet the parents. They demand stuff. They want it now. They use foul language to my principal," reports a St. Louis teacher who made the child–parent behavior connection.[12]

Schools need to be more understanding of the stress facing the modern-day family. But this isn't intended to let parents off the hook, either. If one side wants the other to do the heavy lifting, then it is the child who will fall through the cracks.

Communication and consistency between the home and the school environment will ultimately help create a win-win situation for everybody. If parents really have concerns about school, the parent needs to get in touch with the school sooner rather than later. Like fire prevention, parents cannot wait until the fire is out of control. Parents need to call the fireman (or, in our case, the teacher) before the situation becomes a crisis.

TEACHERS NEED CLASSES IN CLASSROOM MANAGEMENT AND CONTROL

One afternoon an enraged mother pounded on the portable classroom door, demanding entry so she could beat up a child who fought with her daughter earlier that day. Inside, first-year teacher Terri Buckler looked at her class of ten-year-olds, none of whom was any match for an angry mom. "She wasn't trained for this. Reading, writing, math, yes. But not this."[13]

Four-year colleges of education lack classes that focus on how to handle students who misbehave and refuse to admit they're wrong or accept punishment. There are no classes on managing parents—adults—who beat on doors and threaten to hurt children. This would be like the Army not training its soldiers on how to handle guerrilla warfare or fighting terrorists.

Buckler defused the situation with her own problem-solving skills by confronting the angry mother outside the classroom, speaking softly, and promising to right whatever wrong had occurred. In her fourth year of teaching, she has moved on to another middle school where student discipline is less of an issue because of strong administrative support.[14] One approach to helping schools and teachers cope with and get on top of this problem is offered by Pro-Education Media in *Classroom and School Discipline Problems and Prevention*. The classroom management handbook, with faculty/class training video and an independent training CD authored by Howard Seeman, has these key elements:

- A handbook, with its self-improvement exercises, for all the skills needed to implement successful classroom management, and eliminate discipline problems—with a training video and CD both cued to the book—for education workshops, administrators, teachers, and education students.
- The video can be shown at faculty meetings, education workshops, classes, and similar settings, and the CD can be used for independent training at each student or teacher's private computer.
- The video/CD actually demonstrates both ineffective and effective teachers with real classroom discipline problems, demonstrated by real teachers cued to the skills for each section of the book.
- Real teachers spontaneously act out the video/CD display scenes of various discipline problems during enactments in front of actual

students so the viewer can see how real students would respond. If the teacher is effective, then the user sees how real students would actually change their behavior.

The book and video/CD are intended to help educators diagnose the causes of discipline problems, and thereby help with the prevention of disruptive behavior (rather than just controlling discipline problems) for more effective classroom management. The publisher claims it is successfully being used:

- In 400 school districts in public and private schools across the United States.
- In Canadian public and private schools and universities in five provinces.
- In over thirty international schools in Japan, Ghana, Mexico, Malaysia, Greece, Singapore, Switzerland, Iceland, Kuwait, China, and Thailand.

The package has been reviewed by the leading educational publications and periodicals.[15]

TEACHERS ARE NOT AUTOMATICALLY SKILLED IN URBAN STRESS

Student behavior tops the list of classroom concerns. More teachers express the wish they had more basic training in college on how to handle misbehaving students and parents.

Most teaching colleges do not require courses in classroom management or how to control unruly students. But that is *precisely* where the action takes place—in the classroom—and that is why there is increasing stress on the need to learn management of the today's classroom.

"I think that recent issues will require teacher education programs to address the lack of those kinds of courses," said Cynthia Wilson, an associate professor at Florida Atlantic University (FAU) who teaches classroom management to teachers earning degrees in special education. "Kids today will cuss you out to your face. They're not waiting until they leave the classroom."[16]

There's not much room for behavior management classes because colleges now pack so many courses into a teaching degree. FAU and Florida State University introduce behavior and classroom management skills into other classes, but they require specific behavior-related classes only for teachers earning a degree in special education. This is like neglecting to train an airline pilot to handle emergency situations.

The University of Florida now offers the course "Core Classroom Management Strategies" to all teaching students because graduates complained they were unprepared for the tug-of-war in the public school classrooms. Before that, teaching students received bits and pieces here and there, but not in one specific class.

Obviously, teachers want to teach, not control behavior. But part of being a teacher, at least in 2002, is teaching social skills. Teacher complaints about student discipline are not just a matter of the "Oh, these kids today" complex. There is no question that the kind of behavior teachers now see wasn't there ten to fifteen years ago.

Even some first-grade teachers have reported students who have cussed them out. Aggravating the behavior problems are larger societal issues that are out of the control of school boards and teachers.

First, classes are larger. Second, students are coming from many different cultures with different languages. More than a hundred different languages and dialects are spoken in U.S. schools, and more than fifty just in Palm Beach County schools, as an example.[17] Third, movies and video games, which outsold all movie tickets in 2001, are geometrically more violent. Teen parents are more prolific and homes are less disciplined because one or both parents are working, or only one parent is responsible for child rearing.

Teachers and administrators can only accomplish so much in the school. If the behavior is modeled at home and accepted at home, it ties the teacher's hands. The fact is, no matter how good the teacher's skills are, there is always a student (or more than one student) who has trouble with self-control or is overly assertive.

Most teachers would claim they are working very hard with their students on discipline, but they just haven't been given the tools to do it right. There is no doubt that classroom management needs to be much higher on the teaching agenda.

THE CAREER ACADEMY

The oldest question school kids have asked their parents and a teacher is, "Why do I need to go to school?"

A career academy is a high school program in which a group of students stay together with the same teachers for two, three, or four years. Typically, about fifty students are enrolled at each grade level. The curriculum organizes instruction in academic subjects around an industry or occupational theme and this enables the student to fulfill requirements for college entrance in addition to acquiring work-related knowledge and skills.

Academy teachers work together as a team to coordinate teaching in different subjects, stay in touch with parents, and involve employers who support academies in various ways, including provision of adult mentors and internships for students.

Career academies have grown in popularity in recent years, and now operate in hundreds of high schools across the nation. Federal or state laws do not define career academies that spread through local school or business initiatives. The term is applied to very different kinds of programs, and this has created some confusion and the danger that some academies will be created without key elements that effective career academies require.

Several leading networks of career academies have joined for the first time in agreeing on a common standard. Three versions of this definition have been developed to meet the needs of various users and all include the same consensus definition:

- A small learning community, comprising a group of students within the larger high school who take classes together for at least two years, taught by a team of teachers from different disciplines;
- A college preparatory curriculum with a career theme, enabling students to see relationships among academic subjects and their application to a broad field of work;
- Partnerships with employers, the community, and local colleges, bringing resources from outside the high school to improve student motivation and achievement.
- Career academies differ from traditional academic and vocational education because they are intended to prepare high school students for *both* college and careers.

- The academy provides broad information about a field such as health care, finance, engineering, media, or natural resources. They weave this theme into an academic curriculum that qualifies students for admission to a four-year college or university.
- Studies have found that students in career academies perform better in high school and are more likely to continue into postsecondary education, compared to similar students in the same schools. The simple reason is that their first question—"Why?"—is answered in practical terms.

Classroom-to-Career Connection

The career academy high school model integrates school-to-work as classroom-to-career elements in a personalized learning environment. Academies were originally designed as a lifeline for students at risk of dropping out. In 2000, more than 1,500 career academies in the United States serve a broad cross-section of students preparing for college and work.[18]

All the academies share the three essential features: (1) a school within a school, where a cluster of students typically stays with the same group of teachers for two to four years, (2) partnerships with employers who sponsor career awareness and work-based learning opportunities and provide resources and financial support, and (3) an integrated academic and occupational curriculum centered on a career theme, occupation, or industry to provide focused, situational learning.

The goal is to achieve better student engagement and academic performance, student personal and academic development, student preparation for college and work, student postsecondary attainment, and successful student postclassroom employment. Both research and anecdotal evidence show a number of positive outcomes in terms of attendance, grades, credits earned, and graduation rates.

The main goals of career academies are to prevent students from dropping out and to prepare them for college and careers. In 1993, the Manpower Demonstration Research Corporation (MDRC) began conducting the Career Academies Evaluation, a ten-year longitudinal study of the academy model in nine schools around the country. In the evaluation, more than 1,700 academy applicants in the eighth or ninth grade were randomly assigned to enroll in their high school academy (the academy group) or to enroll in any other high school program (the non-academy group). The differences between the two groups' outcomes serve as estimates of the academies' effects.

Owing to its random assignment design, diverse students and sites, and long follow-up period extending four years beyond the students' scheduled high school graduation, the study is both more comprehensive and more rigorous than previous studies of academies and other school reforms. The U.S. Department of Education and Department of Labor as well as seventeen private foundations fund the study.

The impact findings presented in the report are based on survey data collected about one year after scheduled high school graduation. A later report will present results for the rest of the follow-up period.

Evidence of Effectiveness: Some Key Findings

Although participating career academies improved the high school experiences of students in ways consistent with the reform's short-term goals, these positive effects did not translate into changes in high school graduation rates or initial transitions to postsecondary education and jobs.[19]

Earlier results from evaluations indicated that while academies did improve student high school experiences, including participation, the rate at which academic and career-related courses were combined, and the rate at which students participated in career awareness and work-related learning activities, the academies had little influence on course content and classroom instructional practices and left standardized test scores unchanged.

For high-risk students entering the programs, the academies did increase the likelihood of their staying in school through the end of the twelfth-grade year, improved attendance, and increased the number of graduation credits.

The report showed that, relative to similar students nationally, both the academy and the nonacademy groups had high rates of high school graduation, college enrollment, and employment.

The academies had little or no impact on high school graduation rates and initial postsecondary education and employment outcomes. In other words, the nonacademy group matched the academy group's relatively high outcome levels, the best benchmark against which to compare the academy group's performance. This was true for subgroups of students at high, medium, and low dropout risk.

Results suggest that career academies should consider expanding their efforts to recruit students who may not be motivated to enroll in academies on their own, to provide college counseling from the beginning of high school, and to ensure that teachers have access to professional development opportunities aimed at improving curriculum and instruction.

The new findings go beyond those previously presented in earlier reports and from previous research on career academies, but the full story of academies and their effectiveness is still unfolding. Data collected as evaluations continue will shed light on differences between the academy and nonacademy groups' education and labor market experiences that emerge during the second, third, and fourth years after high school.

Some Conclusions

Supporting the three key elements that differentiate career academies is crucial, calling for continuing effort and commitment from teachers, administrators, employers, and students. Successful career academies:

- Adapt to local needs and circumstances, including the role and scope of employer involvement. They successfully keep students in school longer and because enrollment is voluntary, peers, teachers, and families help influence student choice.
- Build up the chances of students graduating by improving attendance and credit accumulation. They have teachers who are satisfied with the quality of their work life because the view of their work environment is shaped by the conditions of the academy. Such an institution helps form a cohesive culture and is most effective when it includes tighter school-within-a-school structure and core groups of academy-only teachers.
- Do not solve all the problems of a high school but prove to be an effective means of enhancing the learning and chances of student graduation. They demonstrate a well-defined approach to creating a more supportive high school environment and increased expo-

sure to career-related learning by serving a heterogeneous population, including high-risk students who seem to benefit the most with those who are already highly engaged.

The support of the learning community is necessary for retention and engagement but not sufficient to improve academic achievement, as measured by standardized tests. Alternative assessments may be more appropriate, but the career academy model demonstrates that doing things slightly different is not enough when it comes to educational reform. To have a real, long-lasting impact on all students, high schools must become dramatically different.[20]

NOTES

1. Shannon Colavecchio and Kimberly Miller, *Palm Beach Post* (April 14, 2002).

2. Colavecchio and Miller.

3. Colavecchio and Miller.

4. Colavecchio and Miller.

5. Colavecchio and Miller.

6. Shannon Colavecchio and Mary Ellen Flannery, *Palm Beach Post* (April 15, 2002).

7. Allen Salowe and Leon Lessinger, *Healing Public Schools: The Winning Prescription to Cure Its Chronic Illness* (Lanham, Md.: Scarecrow Education Press, 2001).

8. Colavecchio and Flannery.

9. Ann Duffet, Jean Johnson, and Steve Farkas, "Kids These Days '99: What Americans Really Think about the Next Generation." *Public Agenda*, 1999.

10. Jean Johnson, Ann Duffett, Steve Farkas, and Kathleen Collins. "Sizing Things Up: What Parents, Teachers and Students Think about Large and Small High Schools." *Public Agenda,* 2002.

11. Mary Ellen Flannery and Kimberly Miller, *Palm Beach Post* (April 15, 2002).

12. Steve Farkas and Jean Johnson, "Aggravating Circumstances: A Status Report on Rudeness in America," *Public Agenda,* New York, 2002.

13. Kimberly Miller, *Palm Beach Post* (April 14, 2002).

14. Miller.

15. Additional information can be obtained from jmanor@suffolk.lib.ny.us who maintains a website at www.panix.com.

16. Miller.

17. Miller.

18. J. J. Kemple, *Career Academies: Communities of Support for Students and Teachers: Emerging Findings from a Ten-Site Evaluation*. (New York: Manpower Demonstration Research Corporation, 1997).

19. Kemple, *Career Academies*.

20. C. Winger and A. Barber, "Career Academies" in *Promising Practices for Connecting High School to the Real World*, edited by W. E. Blank and S. Harwell, 117–122. (Tampa: University of South Florida, 1997).

9

LEVERAGING WHAT WE KNOW

Each day, teachers and other staff drag a ball and chain of interdependent problems into the local school. Russell Ackoff, systems theorist and cyberneticist, termed this situation a "mess," meaning that no one problem can be solved independently of another.

The best we can do with conventional problems is to solve them one by one, but what can be done with a mess? The best we can do is to successfully *manage* a mess. This means attending to one central piece of the puzzle carefully and then seeing what happens to the other pieces.

Puzzles display a series of interlocked pieces that are held together by external pressures. External pressures, for the most part, are outside our control but each pressure still plays a major role. In the case of schools, these external pressures have an effect on how the local school does its jobs and sets its goals.

The literature of change is filled with the simplistic notion that one first diagnoses a system of any kind and then intervenes to change it. Such a thinking model perpetuates a basic error.[1] The theoretical error is that separating the idea of *diagnosis* from the idea of *intervention* ultimately leads to the answer. The distinction comes to us from science where a greater separation exists between the researcher and the researched. It is particularly true in medicine where the physical

THE PUZZLE OF STRUCTURAL CHANGE
(Learning to Manage the Mess)

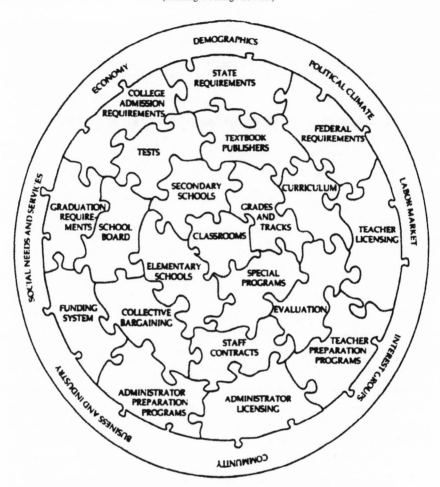

From Russell Ackoff: Technically, a mess is a set of independent problems, no one of which can be solved independently of the others. Problems may be solved; one can only manage messes. To manage a mess successfully, attend to one central piece of the puzzle carefully and then see what happens to the other pieces.

dimensions have long been assumed to be independent of the psychological. As many of us now know, however, this assumption is increasingly out of favor in many parts of medicine.[2]

The classical model, a fairly linear process, is that the doctor makes an examination, runs tests, decides what is wrong, and writes a prescription with recommendations for therapy or, if necessary, surgery.

The educator follows this same model by proposing that a major part of most projects be a diagnostic phase in which large numbers of observations and tests are made as the basis of a set of recommendations given to the student or parent. And now, education standards increasingly require that the school and teachers be held accountable for the implementation of the recommendations and the outcomes of the effort.[3]

WE CANNOT UNDERSTAND A SYSTEM UNTIL WE TRY TO CHANGE IT

Long-term change requires understanding, but we cannot understand a system until we try to change it. So how is it possible to make an adequate diagnosis without intervening?

Kurt Lewin is universally recognized as the founder of modern social psychology. He pioneered the use of theory, using experimentation to test hypotheses. He exposed the world to the significance of an entire discipline—group dynamics and action research.

Lewin conducted many research studies to understand social problems and his concept of "field theory" developed from this approach. To paraphrase his work, human interactions are driven by the people involved *and* their environment. He focused particular attention on the interactions among races and the influences that affect intergroup and intragroup relations. Ultimately, he wanted to identify the factors that could make diverse communities (like schools) function without prejudice and discrimination. Another area of his research was finding out why many groups are so unproductive. His work continues at the Massachusetts Institute of Technology (MIT).

Perhaps his best-known work is developing "force-field analysis" using force-field diagrams. The classic force-field diagram is the "tug-of-war" between forces surrounding a given issue. The tug-of-war taking place within the classroom between teacher and students is a prime example. The tug-of-war between Israel and the Palestinians offers another example.

Using the force-field diagram in education, we would take the "Puzzle of Structural Change" diagram and remove the interlocking segments of the puzzle pieces. Then, we would estimate the give-and-take pressures between the various parts, both adjacent or elsewhere in the puzzle. The force fields that are taking place *between* the parts are *never* static, as they would be in a fixed-cut puzzle. They are in an ever-changing relationship; the pieces are always dynamic and in a state of "push-pull" change. The categories are constantly having a tug-of-war with one another; that is, they compete for greater recognition, more budget, greater importance, more power, more influence, and a host of other powerful psychological and sociological forces.

It quickly becomes clear that in the case of the local school we are dealing with something far more complex than a simple mess. We are dealing with the components of a large system that is a constantly moving and changing shape. The idea is to begin to understand and to make clear and unambiguous the forces acting on each other on any given issue.

FIRST, WE NEED FOCUS

Until this point, we have concentrated attention on how the uncertainties of a free-market global economy can be expected to impact today's students, who are only a few short years away from being tomorrow's workers. We have introduced the recurring doubts flowing from a dynamically changing world. Such external circumstances drive the student's need for ever-changing knowledge and lifelong skills.

Earlier, we focused on the economy because history repeatedly shows the influence that jobs and quality of life have on changing our schools. We subscribe to the old adage, "Those who do not understand history are doomed to repeat it."

The frames that bind our mess together are the social and economic needs of a new world of knowledge work, with a focus on:

1. A dynamic world
2. Business and industry
3. Social needs and services
4. Interest groups and the political climate
5. Community

In a *dynamic world*, changing demographics put our traditional ways of thinking to the new domestic test. Visitors from the Middle East shake our sense of internal security. Our balance of ethnic diversity is fast tilting towards a larger Hispanic population, already increasingly dominating three of our largest states—California, Texas, and Florida.

More competition for jobs comes from immigrant families settling in the United States or using satellite and Internet technology to do the work from remote locations. It comes from Asia, India, Iran, Latin America, Eastern and Western Europe, and the African continent.

People come here from all over the world. They bring with them the common desire to grab their piece of the American dream—a good job, good pay, and a better quality of life than where they came from. Many of these cultures bring with them a built-in family bias toward the value of education. This is especially true for families from India, Japan, and other Far Eastern cultures.

What the newcomers find when they get to America are tens of thousands of students and workers who take for granted our nation's economic health and vitality. What they also find are many American students and their parents who look down on the teachers and the local school.

In the workplace, the newcomers discover that when the jobs call for knowledge and skills, they are more than willing to learn those. The go-getters get out and go get 'em.

American *business and industry* face ever-changing needs as each day they are forced to compete on a more complex global playing field for customers, for their share of market, for new partners, for qualified and cost efficient labor, for materials and services, for financing, and for process improvements.

Producers of American products and services find they must increasingly meet new and demanding international quality and performance standards, such as those promulgated by ISO 9000-2000. This simple idea is so impressive that companies in 110 countries now use the ISO standards. Today, there are more than 13,000 individual series standards used worldwide from Albania to Zimbabwe. As an example, ISO 14000 is the series standard for environmental compliance. It is estimated that over 200,000 auto industry ISO 9000 registrations cover everything from windshield wipers to engines made worldwide.

The bar is constantly being raised on American products, American service quality, and in turn, American worker performance. Quality is in the eye and in the wallet of the customer. This is one of the principle global pressures that the local school must help each student meet.[4]

The global labor market keeps raising the standards for *social needs and services*. Employers need ready-to-go workers who can be immediately productive. The cost of remedial training—going back and fixing the shortcomings of deficient student learning that has been accumulated over years of schooling—is simply too great in both time and dollars.

At the same time, America and its schools face increasing demands to improve health and hammer students with an understanding of American culture and norms, and to do so while teaching English to students coming here from all over the globe speaking upwards of a hundred different languages. Palm Beach County, Florida, schools reportedly have fifty different dialects to contend with.

The number of students with limited English skills, most of them Hispanic, doubled to five million between 1992 and 2002, according to estimates from the U.S. Department of Education. The wave of immigrants during this period, particularly in rural areas far from traditional urban immigration hubs, has left local school districts across the country desperately short of people qualified to teach them English.

The number of qualified teachers for bilingual or English-as-a-second-language (ESL) classes is already in chronically short supply. Market Data Retrieval, a group that keeps national education statistics, estimates 50,000 such teachers in the United States, or one for every 100 students with limited English skills.

This means if students with limited English skills were to be taught in classes of the average national size—about seventeen pupils per teacher—up to 290,000 teachers would be needed for them, said Dr. Marcelo Suarez-Orozco, a Harvard education professor and an expert on immigrant children.

It's a national issue and perhaps most surprisingly, the need for ESL teachers has grown most rapidly in school districts in the South, Midwest, and Northwest. North Carolina, whose farms and factories have drawn thousands of Latino immigrants in recent years, has had the fastest growth of students with limited English skills. The number of such students in the state has more than quintupled since 1993, from 8,900 to 52,500. The population of such students has tripled in Idaho, Nebraska, Alabama, Tennessee, South Carolina, and Georgia since 1993.[5]

Educators now realize that this is no longer just a blip on the map; in fact, the search for solutions appears to be increasingly counterintuitive. For example, the urgency of teacher searches is compounded by the new federal legislation requiring students with limited English skills to take standardized assessment tests by spring 2003. Most states currently exempt such students, and to include their scores with those of other students could drag down a local school's performance, with potentially dire consequences. The Leave No Student Behind Act allows parents to remove their children from schools designated as failing, thus moving state and local dollars with them. Schools with significant numbers of students with limited English skills, therefore, might be designated as failing only because of the language barrier.

Students of English as a second language study subjects like math, science, and social studies in English, often in regular classrooms, while learning English intensively for a few periods a day, tutored in individual or small-group pull-out sessions. Students in bilingual classes are taught the subjects in their native languages. Because it is difficult to find people able to teach subjects in other languages outside the nation's immigrant hubs, few states are able to offer true bilingual education.

Some people think these children of immigrants shouldn't be here and we should send them back to where they came from. The reality is, they are going to stay—and if they are going to stay, the local school will have to educate their children.

Seeing the increasing likelihood that every teacher at some point will encounter a student for whom English is a second language, a small number of principals now require all their teachers to take some ESL education classes. Some districts provide logistical support to the classroom teacher by telephone to an ESL specialist.

The pace of current life and aggressive international competition unfortunately doesn't leave us much slack time to retrain someone just out of high school to think more clearly, write more accurately, and calculate correctly. Let's face it—a grade-C student just isn't good enough in today's world. The military puts it another way. How many of us would want to be stuck in a foxhole in battle with a soldier who is only a grade-D marksman?

Interest groups and the political climate are there to meet their own needs. Some argue to put the Ten Commandments back on the wall or to allow prayer in the classroom or before a high school football game. Teach sex. Don't teach sex. Emphasize more sports and after-school activities. Cut down on sports and after-school activities. Promote school choice. No, forget school choice. The list of push-pull issues seems almost endless.

First interest groups tug the school in this direction, then they tug it in the opposite direction. The beneficial role played by many interest groups soon becomes diluted and even distorted when linked with the political climate. School leaders often develop an aversion to action; they become gun-shy to try anything different.

There is hardly a teacher or administrator who would disagree that the school and classroom could stand some improvement, but the mindset of "the flavor of the month" idea or "here we go again" with some new unproven idea pervades the experience of those educators who have been around the barn a few times.

The local *community* is a window on the global economy. Today's local school must ready the students for unimaginable adaptations— over their school life during the next twenty years or over a lifetime.

The local community's needs are also pressing. It must promote and maintain a vibrant local economy to help ensure a strong tax base and, at the same time, help bring about a healthy environment for families and business. Everyday matters such as public safety, fire protection, roads and bridges, fresh drinking water, sewers to carry away wastewater, and drainage to prevent flooding round out just a few of the community's "basic" needs.

To summarize our focus, it's this: The public sees the most important purpose of the public school is to prepare each student to be a responsible citizen and to help each student become *economically self-sufficient*. In simple terms, parents want to see their child live the American dream.

WHERE WE START

What holds this mess together? The outer ring is made up of many conflicting goals. The objectives aim our fire in many different directions.

We are trying to help change the processes of K–12 schools—to change "the way things are done around here"—in order to better prepare teachers with methods to help students handle the future uncertainties of a twenty-first-century knowledge economy. By concentrating on process improvements, the educator automatically arrives at student improvement. At the end of the day, the K–12 school experience offers greater opportunities for the next generation.

Our Vision . . . to Be a TQ Team!

1. Care about each other.

2. Believe the leader who is proud and cares for us.

3. Come to learn skills we can really use.

4. Trust our judgments.

5. Make good decisions.

6. Don't say, "I can't."

7. Learn from our mistakes.

8. Solve our own problems.

9. Make good choices.

10. Don't spread rumors.

11. Be serious about meeting our goals.

12. Have fun and laugh a lot.

13. Keep on trying . . . persevere.

14. Be the best that we can be.

15. We're not perfect, but we always try to improve.

16. Make our bosses and customers happy.

Before delving into the puzzle, let's ask Mrs. Edwards' first-grade class to paraphrase some practical guidance, this time from the children's perspective.

EXAMINE THE PUZZLE CAREFULLY

On any given day, the local school grapples with most puzzle parts, so the key question becomes: Where can we find the points of greatest leverage to positively move other parts? We cannot discard any of the parts. We want to move as many parts as possible in the direction of student improvement. If we were to survey teachers and administrators at any given hour, they would most likely give us different answers.

Teachers and administrators are effective firefighters and they have mastered handling emergencies as a daily happening. The common question is, where's the fire and what's burning today? A good guess might be controlling and motivating student behavior.

There are lots of examples of unacceptable student behavior but one underlying question has unnerved kids for years about school. "What am I learning all this stuff for? Why can't I just get out in the world and learn as I go?"

Thirty percent of seventeen-year-olds decide each year to skip their high school education and get on with it, whatever *it* is. That means there is merit and immediacy in the student's question that parents and educators have been unwilling to face.

WHY ARE WE HERE?

More than delivering more work-ready students to the community and the workplace, CTC answers this central question. A cooperative CTC program gives students a defined purpose—a reason—to be in school and to perform well in classes, specifically in their chosen apprenticeship. This holds true for all children, including those who are physically or mentally challenged.

The CTC focus melds neatly with the "Three-R" curriculum. The student learns to apply the "basics" and other disciplines "on the job" in the real world. The better the students learn on the job and perform the assigned tasks, the greater their chances of developing critical thinking—a bridge to future opportunity.

The CTC approach gets everyone past the "burger-flipping" career-track threat (unless, of course, the student decides to enroll in the field of hotel, restaurant, and resort management covered earlier, which eventually rewards strong performers for delivering quality food, services, and lodging).

CTC shortens the time horizon of students anxious to get on with "practical" matters. Today's youngster is more precocious, more curious, and exposed to more good and more not-so-good stuff beyond the classroom and living room. CTC helps relieve the teacher from continuously pressing to convince the student that "being good today will pay off tomorrow."

THE DEMING EFFECT

Following World War II, W. Edwards Deming was so instrumental in fostering the "Japanese economic miracle" that Japan's highest honor today is the Deming Medal. He insisted that the core of improving school processes is the *prevention* of student failure and reduced need for student remediation. Do it right the first time, and we don't need to do it over.

Deming's goal was not to discover defects but rather to find the knowledge and insights needed to improve the processes that lead to defects. This means eliminating problems *before* they lead to undesirable consequences. Deming stresses fire prevention rather than waiting for firefighting. The guts of what he gave us is this: "Ninety-four percent of the troubles an organization has can be attributed to system. Only 5 percent are due to [what he terms] special causes." This kind of thinking replaces finger pointing and in its place offers critical guidance. It is a simple and direct fix. Focus on *fixing the processes* and the end result takes care of itself.

"Made in America" needs to become a point of pride, especially for schools. And what schools must turn out is the highest caliber citizen and societal contributor possible. The route to achieving this, in part, is to bring *quality* principles and process methods into education.[6]

We've been aware of school problems for a long time. The question is: What must we *really* do about it to ensure that it is fixed—and fixed for the long term?

TQM—Mrs. Edwards' Class

Total quality management (TQM) is the daddy of America's quality efforts to improve products and services. TQM starts with a vision. Mrs. Edwards' first-grade class spells out what we mean by quality at its most basic.

Quality is increasingly the hallmark of workplace performance. Students and teachers need to master these simple principles if they are to make it in an uncertain free-market global economy.

ISO 9000

The International Organization for Standardization, begun shortly after World War II, is headquartered in Geneva, Switzerland. It takes its name from the Greek word *iso* meaning *equal* (for example, an *iso*sceles triangle has equal sides).

Today, the format of all credit cards, phone cards, ATM, and "smart" cards are commonplace and derive from an ISO international standard. The standard defines such features as optimal thickness (0.76mm). It means that these cards are usable worldwide. International standards contribute to making life simpler, and to increasing the reliability and effectiveness of the goods and services we use. It assures reliability through consistency.

A box of photographic film with ISO 200 guarantees the 200-speed film meets an international standard of quality (ISO) and fits any camera that takes that size film. It is the voluntary agreement among 110 nations that ensures the ATM card and cash machine will dispense your money request anywhere in the world. ISO standards ensure that a music CD or DVD works reliably in a ready machine anywhere in the world. The list is almost endless.

In 1987, ISO issued its first series of standards for service enterprises like schools. Underlying ISO standards is quality process assurance to help satisfy customers. Conformance with standards helps ensure reduced specification failures during a product's manufacturing or service delivery. ISO 9000-2000 is a simplified outline essentially aimed at education standards.

Great Britain was first to embrace ISO standards for schools and colleges. Now, nations as disparate as Singapore, Israel, and Thailand have followed suit within their school systems. U.S. schools are gradually joining in and Lancaster, Pennsylvania, was the first school district to display the "ISO Registered" banner. Several other U.S. school districts are in the registration pipeline. Dr. Vicki Phillips, superintendent of the Lancaster district, contributed the foreword to this book.

Baldrige Quality Program

Ronald Reagan signed into law the Malcolm Baldrige National Quality Award Act in 1987. The Baldrige is acknowledged as key to the improvement and continued success of U.S. business globally.

Local school districts now use Baldrige as a quality stimulus. Over half the school districts in North Carolina are presently using the Baldrige program. New Jersey passed legislation equating meeting Baldrige criteria with having satisfied state education standards. Tennessee has made a major commitment to Baldrige in education.

Forty-four states have quality award programs based on Baldrige. The Baldrige Criteria for Education is "a new culture" in itself. It prescribes a new way of doing things: It focuses the school on the customer, aligns internal processes with customer needs, gets school staff to work on shared goals, promotes continuous improvement, demands management by fact, sponsors prevention rather than reaction, looks for ways to be more responsive, finds partnering opportunities, and values results.

This Baldrige Quality Stuff Really Works

On March 7, 2002, U.S. Commerce Secretary Don Evans announced that for the eighth consecutive year the "Baldrige Index" outperformed the Standard and Poor 500 (S&P 500) stock average.

The Baldrige Index is a fictitious stock fund comprised of publicly traded U.S. companies receiving the Baldrige Quality Award between

1991 and 2000. "Even after a tough year for the stock market, especially for technology stocks, the Baldrige Index continues to make a terrific showing, outperforming the S&P 500 for the eighth year. While performance in the stock market is only one indicator of success, this study and others show that businesses that seek excellence in everything they do can achieve success in many areas, including the bottom line," said Evans.[7]

The National Institute of Standards and Technology (NIST) manages the Baldrige program. Here's how the index test worked. The index supposedly "invested" $1,000 in each of the whole company winners—Eastman Chemical Company (1993 winner) and Solectron Corp. (1991 and 1997 winner)—and the parent companies of eighteen subsidiary winners. Another hypothetical $1,000 was invested in the S&P 500 for the same time period. The results were revealing.

The two whole-company winners outperformed the S&P 500 by almost 4.5 to 1—a 512 percent return on investment. The group of whole-company winners plus the parent companies of subsidiary winners outperformed the S&P 500 by about 3 to 1—a 323 percent return on investment. This compares with a 110 percent return for the S&P 500 alone. All of the investments were tracked from the first business day of the month following the announcement of award recipients through December 3, 2001. Adjustments were made for stock splits.

Receiving a Baldrige Award or any other award is no guarantee of success but it is a strong indicator of advanced management thinking. To win the award, organizations demonstrate continuous and major improvements following the program criteria. For example:

- Solectron Corp. has received more than 400 quality and service awards from its customers, in addition to being the only two-time winner of the Baldrige National Quality Award. Founded in 1977, the company had revenue of $265 million with 1,500 employees. In 2001, Solectron revenue was $18 billion with 60,000 employees.
- Federal Express Corp. won a Baldrige Award in 1990; the company had revenues of $7 billion with 90,000 employees, and 1.5 million shipments a day. In 2001, Federal Express revenues were $19.6 billion, over 215,000 employees handling 5 million shipments a day.

Other studies also show that organizations receiving quality awards gain long-lasting improvements. Studies at Georgia Institute of Technology together with the University of Western Ontario studied 600 publicly traded firms that had won quality awards, including the Baldrige. The five-year study showed these firms improved in many areas, including stock price return, operating income, and sales.

The Baldrige National Quality Program is a public–private partnership. Awards are made to organizations that have substantially benefited the economic or social well-being of the United States through improvements in performance excellence. Awards are given in five categories: manufacturing, service, small business, education, and health care.

The Baldrige helps develop and promote measurements, standards, and technology to enhance productivity, facilitate trade, and improve the U.S. quality of life.

Baldrige Teaches Students and Their Teachers

A closer look at Solectron, the world's largest electronics manufacturing services (EMS) company offering a full range of integrated supply-chain solutions for the world's leading electronics original equipment manufacturers (OEM) tells us much about the success of quality programs.

The company received more than 400 quality and service awards in addition to the 1997 and 1991 Malcolm Baldrige National Quality Awards, the first company to win the Baldrige Award for manufacturing twice in the history of the national program.

- For students, it clearly signals that all of the Solectron's 60,000 employees must be quality conscious, quality driven, and grasp how following quality standards results in higher levels of performance. This is not a guessing game. It is not a practice of "whatever" as an answer. It is more than just common sense.
- For teachers, it says that understanding and applying quality principles is a discipline of thinking and control management. It is spreading throughout the workplace so every student needs to learn the basics, even if that means we periodically go back to Mrs. Edwards' first-grade class vision for a twelfth-grade class.

Solectron provides integrated services to the world's leading OEMs and is well known for its printed circuit board assembly (PCBA). It delivers a full range of services to customers in a variety of industries. Which of the following industries is most likely to tolerate low standards or quality as its employee, product, and service motto?

- Automotive, including onboard audio and navigation systems, antilock brake systems, and supplemental restraint controls?
- Computer docking stations, Internet access devices, mainframes, midrange servers, notebooks, PC servers, PCs, retail systems, supercomputers, and workstations?
- Consumer electronics such as set-top boxes, video game consoles?
- Computer peripherals, including disk and tape drives, the fax machine, laser and inkjet printers?
- Networking hubs, modems, remote access, routers, and switching?
- Telecommunication equipment, base stations, IP telephone equipment, mobile phones and pagers, switching, transmission, and video conferencing equipment?
- Others including avionics, medical electronics, semiconductor equipment, and test/industrial controls?

Solectron operates in sixteen states, six Canadian provinces, Mexico, fifteen European countries, four Caribbean islands, three nations in South America, and eight Asia/Pacific nations. Solectron analyzes a product's design, materials, processes, and testing methods to ensure manufacturing efficiency and lowest total cost in the supply chain. A centralized supply-base management structure, in conjunction with local site commodity teams, enables the company to provide the global leverage in total cost, supply assurance, local responsiveness, flexibility, and time to volume that its customers require to compete in the global marketplace.

What would it take for one of your students to work for Solectron or one of its partners?

Not interested in high tech? Look at Baldrige winner Federal Express:

- "Most Admired Global Companies," 7th (*Fortune* March 2002)
- "America's Most Admired Companies," 8th (*Fortune* February 2002)

- "8th in Corporate Reputation" (RQ Gold Survey: January 2002)
- "100 Best Companies to Work for in America" (*Fortune* 1998–2002)
- "50 Best Companies for Minorities" (*Fortune* July 2001)
- "Top CEOs list Frederick W. Smith" (*Forbes* 2001)
- "Asia's Leading Companies," 24th in 2000, 6th in 2001 (*Far Eastern Economic Review*)
- "Top 35 Companies to Work for in Canada" (*Globe & Mail* 2001)
- Ranked 25th "Top 25 Companies to Work for in Canada" (Hewitt Association 2001)
- Ranked 11th among top 20 employers in Puerto Rico (Hewitt Association, Price Waterhouse Coopers, and *El Nuevo Día*, March 2001)

FedEx needs its 200,000-plus delivery and pickup persons, package handlers, schedulers, customer relationship persons, truck and plane maintenance personnel, pilots, and on and on, to be proficient in high-tech skills, accuracy, and dependability. Learning both on the job and in the classroom opens a world of opportunities for students.

OUTER-RING PIECES LINK WITH CLASSROOM-TO-CAREER INITIATIVES

The "rules and regs" of teaching and learning—those vital components shown in the outer ring of our puzzle—need to be linked to classroom-to-career programs. The outer ring of our puzzle includes:

- State requirements
- Federal requirements
- Teacher licensing
- Teacher preparation programs
- Administrator licensing
- A funding system
- Graduation requirements
- College admission requirements

State requirements still mostly focus on nineteenth-century schooling rather than twenty-first-century methods and standards. The CTC initiative expands the burden of measurement to today's "real world" application of mandatory subject learning.

Federal requirements mostly concentrate on protecting and ensuring student civil rights. In 2002, the Leave No Child Behind Act concentrated on accountability in the classroom and school building. Regrettably, neither effort goes to the root of preparing kids for thinking and succeeding in an Information Age.

Teacher licensing is moving toward tighter requirements while the profession begs for new teachers and struggles to hang on to its most experienced teachers. Teachers and students need the sharper focus of CTC to help make expected improvements.

Teacher preparation programs are many, but General Motors puts more hours per year into training someone building Saturn automobiles than a school district provides to teachers—and the teacher's work is a lot more important in the long term than building quality cars.

Every classroom is a tough neighborhood, so teachers need tough basic training. We have a more demanding knowledge world and that isn't likely to change much in the foreseeable future.

The management processes within which the typical teacher works are badly outmoded. Teachers need hands-on, personal exposure to workplace experiences so that they can better understand the employer's needs and then translate these into better-prepared students. Being a good citizen includes being a good worker.

Administrator licensing is badly outdated. Running a school is the job of a professional manager, not just an educator-administrator. In CTC, administrators build bridges to the community workplace, not just remain up to date on testing, personnel, curriculum, and behavior.

Funding systems are badly broken. The local property owner-taxpayer is stretched beyond limits and being asked to pay more for less, to pay more school taxes for poorer-performing schools. State funding programs and federal funding programs contribute to a hodge-podge of "let's try this and then let's try that" experimentation.

A disciplined process is needed to improve student and teacher performance by linking CTC programs to all grades. Simply stated, here are the five straightforward continuous improvement performance management methods that work best.

1. Say what you're going to do.
2. Write down what you said you'll do.
3. Do it.
4. Measure what you said you'd do.
5. Learn from your mistakes.

Then start this never-ending continuous improvement process over from the beginning.

We need to also count the monies wasted, not just the amounts poured into a cost-per-student calculation. Do the arithmetic yourself:

1. If one out of three students does not finish high school, and
2. If one out of three of those who stick it out is poorly prepared for the work place, and
3. Only one out of three students who remain is ready for work, further schooling, or the military, then
4. How many school dollars have been wasted each year when fully two out of three students finish below standard? What is the full cost of preparing one proficient student, including the cost of wasted money?

Graduation requirements are shameful. The number of functionally illiterate graduates turned out and the poor preparation of students for today's workplace (let alone the knowledge economy) scream loudly. Classroom-to-career programs make even more sense.

College admission requirements lack a classroom-to-career focus. The student needs to be helped to develop a plan for further schooling and mentored toward a career. Mentoring is not the same as tracking.

It's no longer acceptable for college-level educators to take the student's (most likely the parent's or student loan) money, sell them textbooks, keep attendance records, play the role of "sage on the stage," book the grades, count the credits, give them a graduation pep talk about the world beyond, and hand out a diploma. Our students deserve a better chance at a satisfying job in the free-market global economy.

THE MIDDLE RING AND CLASSROOM-TO-CAREER INITIATIVES

"Rules and regs" exert their pressures on the classroom and the surrounding ring exerts its push and pull on the entire puzzle. The middle ring imposes "the hidden culture" on the classroom. This ring silently says: "This is the way we do things around here." These puzzle pieces are:

- School board policies
- Collective bargaining and staff contracts
- Evaluation
- Curriculum
- Textbooks
- Tests

School board policies either take into account or have knee-jerk reactions to social and political pressures and, in turn, transfer many of these to the classroom. The school board is faced with the need to provide backbone policies to support educational leadership and bring needed changes and improvements.

Collective bargaining and staff contracts spell out the agreed-upon ground rules for school operations, usually arrived at in a tug-of-war between the board and organizations that represent administrators, teachers, and staff.

Evaluation is the management tool used to promote, reward, or deny employment to tenured and nontenured personnel. The evaluation programs are dictated by due process spelled out in contracts.

Curriculum is supposed to drive *textbooks and tests*—at least, that is what one normally thinks. Just as often, however, textbook selection drives curriculum and tests. Topping it off are mandatory statewide testing requirements to meet federal accountability laws, which puts tests further in the driver's seat pushing textbooks and curriculum in another direction. The tug-of-war is played out—not with the student in mind—but driven by the vested interests of textbook publishers and test publishers. Curriculum, textbooks, and tests bring a three-ring tug-of-war circus to town.

THE RUBBER HITS THE ROAD IN THE INNER CIRCLE

The central question remains, "Has the focus remained on the student?"

The mind-set starts at the elementary school level and Mrs. Edwards helped get us get off on the right foot.

Secondary school students usually show a strong interest in CTC programs. This ties together the practical use of needed basics for the student. It changes the tug-of-war relationship into a win-win game plan. For a change, it puts the teacher and the student on the same team.[8] It gives the student practical demonstrations why accurate mathematics, critical thinking, clear writing skills, and proficiency in reading really count.

AT THE CENTER: THE CLASSROOM

Now, step back for a moment and look at the puzzle. Its fixed links are now gone. Each piece is engaged in a tug-of-war with other pieces. It's easier to see why the classroom is sometimes lost in the "bigger" battles, but it also gives us guidance for how to keep the classroom and student at the center of decision making.

We set out to help change the processes of K–12 schools—to change "the way things are done around here" and to better prepare students for the twenty-first-century knowledge economy. We focused on process improvement so that teachers could better achieve student improvement so that the K–12 school experience benefits more students.

The school classroom and teachers are deeply entrenched. In many ways, schools are the best example of the complacency of this country. We rest on our laurels even as we say we are going to do things differently. Look at the nation's airport security post–September 11. We parade the National Guard brandishing automatic weapons as security. Israel's national airline, El Al, practices security against this same potential terrorism with hidden methods. There is no perfect solution, but at least there are some better and more proven effective answers.

Educators at every level believe in what they do. They are committed to fulfilling the needs of students and assisting in the creation of thinking beings who are intended to become valuable and contributing adults. Otherwise, they couldn't get through the typical school day, let alone the school year.

NOTES

1. See Allen Salowe and Leon Lessinger, *Healing Public Schools: The Winning Prescription to Cure Its Chronic Illness* (Lanham, Md.: Scarecrow Press, 2001) for a more complete discussion of the application of quality processes in schools.

2. See Allen Salowe, *Prostate Cancer: Overcoming Denial with Action* (New York: St. Martins Press, 1998).

3. Salowe, *Prostate Cancer*.

4. Announcement at a presidential ceremony honoring recipients of the 2001 Malcolm Baldrige National Quality Award. March 7, 2002, available at www.nist.gov/public_affairs/factsheet/stockstudy.htm.

5. Yilu Zhao, "Wave of Pupils Lacking English Strains Schools," *New York Times* (August 5, 2002).

6. Salowe and Lessinger, *Healing Public Schools*.

7. Salowe and Lessinger, *Healing Public Schools*.

8. Allen Salowe and Leon Lessinger, *Game Time: The Educator's Playbook for the New Global Economy* (Lancaster, Pa.: Technomic Press, 1997).

10

CLASSROOM-TO-CAREER
PROGRAMS AND THE FUTURE

Shaping the broad picture into a set of executable actions is analytical, and it's a huge intellectual, emotional, and creative challenge.[1]

—*Execution: The Discipline of Getting Things Done*, 2002

Management guru Peter Drucker talks of the time he spent with the human resources people of the twenty largest Japanese corporations. "I had reviewed a list of questions they sent me, and I began by saying there is one important question you have not asked: How will you run a company in fifteen years when the retirement age will be seventy-five?"[2]

Drucker shocked them because most Japanese companies had yet to recognize that their current retirement age was sixty. Japan had been the youngest of the developed countries in the Far East; in 2006, it's going to be the oldest. And there is no way Japan can possibly support all those retired people; even loyal, faithful, obedient Japanese citizens will balk at handing over half their pay to people in reasonably good physical and mental shape.

Similarly, the United States faces the same challenge; today's students are our future.

CLASSROOM-TO-CAREER TIME HORIZON: TWENTY YEARS

It seems hard to believe that in just twenty years, today's grade K–6 students will be driving toward getting a bachelor's degree or already into the early stages of their work careers. Today's grade 7–9 students will be a part of the different kind of workforce that we already see unfolding, with different kinds of pressures. And the grade 10–12 students may be well on the way to becoming grandparents and starting to think about such unimaginable matters as their own retirement. Twenty years passes by quickly.

In the U.S. Congress, the talk is about balancing the budget by year 2010. Unfortunately, by the year 2010 or so, no matter what Congress agrees on—given the present retirement age of sixty-five, let alone an enormous number of early retirements—the nation will be on the verge of total bankruptcy.

If the present trends continue, America will have about 3.3 people in the labor force for every retired person above age sixty-five. We cannot expect this ratio of adults to retirees in the labor force to change. In other words, we're not very likely to send eleven-year-old kids out into the workforce. Since the start of the 1980s, the most privileged segment of the population in all developed countries has been older people in retirement. And it should come as no surprise that older folks become increasingly self-centered as they grow older.

We have a tremendous problem we need to face up to. The world has never had a demographic revolution that came about as fast and as thoroughly as that of the twentieth century. In 1900 or so, nineteen out of twenty people in the entire world did manual work. This was the Industrial Age. Fewer than one in twenty lived in a city with a population over 100,000. Today, somewhere between one in four and one in five of those working in developed countries do manual labor and half the world's people live in cities with over 100,000 persons.

Around 1900, the average work-life span was about twenty-five years. When Social Security went into effect, the average lifespan was only around sixty-five years. That's how the Congress arrived at the payout age for retirees. They simply never expected that most people would live to collect a pension check. The crafters of the nation's retirement programs never dreamed of people living to age seventy-five or eighty-five or even a hundred years of age. A girl born in 2002 has a life expectancy of one hundred years.

We now need to keep people working fifty years—until age seventy-one or so—so they can support themselves and help to maintain a growing and robust economy. It becomes clearer why this same group will need to retool its knowledge and skills several times over. "So, barring another world war, the great political issue in every developed country will be the age issue."[3]

A severe indictment of our organizations is the fact that people, even in well-paid jobs, choose ever-earlier retirement. And this isn't just happening in business, which faces an increasingly pressure-packed global economy. It's happening each school year in teaching, which has always been one of the battlegrounds of social change, and in the universities, which still languish in an outmoded power structure. These are people who no longer find their jobs interesting or challenging.

All of us probably know a neighbor with a fairly responsible position in a major company who has taken early retirement at about age fifty-four and now spends his time golfing, fishing, and driving around in an RV.

In times past, the man who worked in a steel plant and took early retirement at age fifty-five, after thirty-five years on the job, was physically worn out from heavy physical work. This man was probably willing to sit on a pier dangling a fishing line in the water for twenty years—maybe.

Chances are, today's sales manager, attorney, or other professional who worked thirty-five years is not physically worn out. Employers are not facing up to the demand to make knowledge jobs interesting and more challenging. Employers still dumb down the work mainly because it puts so much emphasis on promotion, but promotion is only for one out of ten. A great many employees end up disappointed with their chosen careers and this is a reality of today's and tomorrow's workplace.

The emphasis on promotion is a post–World War II event flowing from earlier demographic changes. "For example, between 1950 and 1975, in the major New York banks, twenty-seven years went from being the length of time you served before being eligible to become a vice president, to being the age at which you could become vice president."[4] Today, both banks and major corporations have armies of vice presidents.

THE TEACHER'S JOB: MAKE THE WORK CHALLENGING

For 150 years, from 1850 on, society moved steadily toward being a society of organizations. In 1900, nobody worked in an "organization." It's a 1950s term first made popular by William Whyte's book *The Organization Man* (1956).

Lots of people were employed—hired hands on the farm, domestic servants, journeymen in their shop—but they worked for a master, not an organization—and the work was very personal. The organization became the organizer, though not necessarily the employer. Now we have all kinds of dangerous liaisons.

One of the things about outsourcing (working for a contract organization), for example, is the woman working for the hospital cleaning floors used to find it a very boring job. But today—if this were an ideal world—if she works for ServiceMaster, an outsourcing company, she is excited by it because people listen to her and people challenge her. She is expected to improve the job and she gets paid for doing just that; whereas before, no one would even listen.

Only five years ago, her supervisor had a broom in her hands. Today, the outsourcing people have a great strength in making what some might call a dead-end job into something much more challenging, because they take it more seriously. We need to see that properly cleaning a hospital is an essential part of keeping the hospital free of infection. It is an integral part of the health provider and delivery system. Unfortunately, we've got a long way to go yet at giving that kind of dignity to every job.

Tomorrow's Organization

The executive may change more than the organization does. The top manager is going to be more like the elder chieftain of the Cherokees. In other words, the top manager will have little authority other than that which flows from wisdom, competence, and accomplishment—but each higher level of management will become increasing accountable for achieving and reporting accurate results.

Today's grade 10–12 students, if they choose to enter the world of business, will need to learn not just how to run a business but how to build a business. That means they will have far fewer employees but heaven only knows how many people who work with them. That is the organization of the future. The term *executive* is used to connote a professional who is in charge of his or her own profession. In this context, a doctor is a professional and an executive. The doctor who has a PA and nurse on the staff does manage them to the extent that they must meet or exceed professional standards, but the "professional manager" of the William Whyte's description in *The Organization Man* is rapidly being replaced by a self-sufficient, knowledgeable, professional executive in charge of meeting his or her own professional standards (ISO/Baldrige/scientific, etc.).

The present people in many organizations, like the local school, remain stuck in the nineteenth-century organization model for the most part. When big business first came upon the scene in the industrial world of 1870, it did not emerge out of the small businesses of 1850. It came about independently.

Drucker often relates the fact that the most successful organization of the nineteenth century was the Prussian army, which had been reorganized. It had learned its lessons from the inability of the Americans in the Civil War, both the North and the South, to organize, move, and communicate with masses of people. It became the first modern organization.

In 1866 the Prussians defeated the Austrians, who had a much larger and better-equipped army; four years later, they went on to defeat the French, who were even better armed. The Prussians succeeded because they had created an organization. They were the first ones to use modern technology effectively, which in those days meant railroad and telegraph.[5]

Business and education copied the command-and-control structure of the Prussian army, in which rank equaled authority. Business and education are still evolving toward structures in which rank means *responsibility* but not authority. In this structure, the job is not to command but to persuade. In this structure, authority is based on expertise and the respect and responsibility that go with it, not on ability to pull rank.

New Relationships Mean More Trust

It starts with a different kind of attitude. We start out with what's best for them, the customer, not what's best for us. We refer to this as customer-focus—or more closely to our central topic, student centered.

Trust means leaders who see themselves not as the boss but as the conductor. Arturo Toscanini was a very autocratic symphony conductor but he did not see himself as the boss. Toscanini saw himself as the servant of the composer and the interpreter of the music score. So too did Leonard Bernstein, Arthur Fiedler, and a long line of other great conductors.

The world's great symphony conductors repeatedly remind us that their job is to make the orchestra hear the score the way the maestro hears it. The conductor may not know how to get a single note out of a French horn but he trusts the French horn player to know how to play the instrument. What the conductor says is, "French horns, I would like to have this a little louder." Or a little slower, or a little softer. That authority rests on the ability of the conductor to share, to communicate.

Trust is built on the conviction that this conductor, this coordinator, this executive, creates a partnership—and then we, the audience, "hear" the trust.

Knowledge workers, those gangly or pudgy kids who come out of today's classrooms, will need to be managed as if they are volunteers. They need expectations, self-confidence, and, above all, a network. This gives them mobility, which is a significant change from the employees of yesterday and today.

Not long ago, the son of a farmer remained a farmer. Even in America, social mobility was almost unknown. Today, every young person has his or her updated résumé on the computer hard drive, which few (if any) blue-collar workers ever did.

In tomorrow's workplace, it needs to be an accepted fact that leaders treat almost anybody as a volunteer. They are knowledge workers and therefore carry their tools in their heads; they can go anywhere. Today's student needs to grasp this fundamental. It's what's in their head that counts most.

What attracts and holds volunteers is a clear mission. People need to know what their organization stands for and is trying to accomplish. These people look for responsibility for results, which means appraisal and review. And they crave continuous learning. Continuous learning!

Practices That Will Still Apply in the Future

In leadership, the first constant is to make human strength effective and human weaknesses irrelevant. That is the purpose of the organization and it is the one thing an organization does that the individual cannot do better.

Another constant is that leaders are accountable for results, period! They are not paid to be philosophers; they are not even being paid for their knowledge. They are paid for results. Leadership is not a branch of philosophy but a practice. The same principle applies to teachers and administrators.

Managers, including school leaders and teachers, must deliver results, and results are not quite as easy to define as they once were in the local school organization. The balance between short term and long term, for instance, remains a constant challenge.

What is expected to remain constant and even more relevant is that people in developed societies will become increasingly dependent on access to an organization. Because they are knowledge specialists, they need access to the specialized knowledge of others in order to do a job. Scientists and engineers need to team not only with other scientists and engineers but also with sociologists, behavior psychologists, accountants, and, yes, teachers.

All schools and local governments, churches and universities, can be expected to become more interdependent, more customer driven. Today it is a world of infinite choices. With churches, it used to be that you were born into a denomination and stayed there. In the fast-growing pastoral churches, which are one of the most significant social developments in America, only 10 percent of the members were born into that denomination. There is acute competition in all authorities.

There will be new monopolies. For example, one institution still controls access to careers and livelihood in a way no earlier society would have—the college and university are major gatekeepers. That's why we have fights about admissions. For better or worse, a branch of First Union Bank or NationsBank is not likely to hire someone who doesn't have a college degree for a training position. It may not make perfect sense or seem fair but that's not the point; it's a fact we need to accept and convey to students.

The Rearview Mirror

U.S. enterprise is not just getting leaner, it's getting meaner. And during the past twenty years, it's also been getting keener. Enterprises have adopted new structures and practices to take advantage of the value-adding capabilities of America's knowledge technologies. Public and private sector employers have taken on productive new arrangements, causing several trends to emerge. This has had a profound effect on workers and on the schools that are charged with preparing workers for this new workplace.

Futurists, notably Bell, Toffler, and Naisbitt, have long forecast these trends.[6] The fact that "long-range" forecasts have now become universal realities is in large measure a powerful indicator of how far into the future we have already traveled.

The social contract that promised job security in exchange for employee loyalty is broken. American companies continue to downsize, restructure, and lay off thousands of workers. Work that is not considered to be part of the "core competency" of the organization is increasingly outsourced or performed by temporary, part-time, or contract workers.

Today, there are twenty-eight million "temps" in the United States, representing over 20 percent of the workforce—up more than 400 percent since 1980, when temps represented only 4.5 percent of all workers (five million people). The upside to this dismal trend is that, as the workplace has "regularized" using contingent workers at all levels of employment—executives to support workers—the pay and benefits of these workers have gradually caught up to full-time wage earners.

This trend is expected to continue since it has become a cost-effective method of increasing and decreasing staffs. It means that many Americans—by some estimates as many as half of the workforce—will be contingent workers employed in part-time, temporary, contract, or other nontraditional employment. This is the picture of the workplace that awaits our grade 6–10 students in just a few precious years.

Many highly skilled workers will be self-employed solo professionals. The other half of the workforce will be employed in full-time permanent jobs where they are expected to behave as continuously adaptive, self-developing team players in exchange for the benefits of career employment.

The number of employees who telecommute or work at nontraditional work sites such as satellite offices is also expected to keep on growing throughout most of the early twenty-first century. Thanks to technology and the changing nature of work itself, more than half the workforce today performs jobs for which physical location is no longer critical.

According to the U.S. Census, at least one out of three American households have one person performing compensated work at home for at least one day per week. Dispersed, "anytime-anywhere" workspace networks are steadily replacing the geographic "same-time-same-place" workplace. Within a few years, the phrase "going to work" will become a relic for most Americans. Work, for them, will be what they do, not the place they go to.

Practically all jobs promise to continue facing "skill creep" as the technical workforce grows in size and importance. Today, there are some 20 million technical workers in the United States. A quarter of all new jobs are technical; workers with strong technical skills—lab technicians, computer professionals, drafters, paralegals, medical technicians, designers, engineers, and so on—are now the front-line workers of most organizations.

Even jobs not traditionally considered technical, such as the job of a courier, now include a strong technical component and require the use of computers and other sophisticated electronic communication devices. The semiskilled and unskilled jobs that once employed masses of illiterate or semiliterate workers in the past are rapidly disappearing.

We can expect to see continued rapid growth in cross-functional and multidisciplinary teams with globally and ethnically diverse memberships. Already, a third of American companies with fifty or more employees have half or more of their employees working in self-managed or problem-solving teams.

Many of these teams have no traditional boss or supervisor. Instead, team members take on responsibility for planning, organizing, staffing, scheduling, directing, monitoring, and controlling their own work. More importantly, these teams are linked via the Internet or other global networks, with unrestricted flows of information within and between teams and team members and among outside suppliers and customers.

Maybe Car Making and Teaching Aren't So Different

Two powerful labor unions—the United Auto Workers (UAW) and the American Federation of Teachers (AFT)—are battling to represent adjunct professors at New York University, a corps of nearly 3,000 part-time teachers at the low end of the academic totem pole, reported the *New York Times* on May 27, 2002.[7]

The contest over a group of instructors, who have largely been ignored at NYU and elsewhere, reflects the role adjuncts increasingly play in the universities and a growing effort to unionize higher education.

"If NYU goes this route, Columbia and other universities won't be far behind," said Jack H. Schuster, professor of education and public policy at Claremont Graduate University in California. "While there are other places where this may be occurring, they will not send the same signal that a place with a reputation like NYU will."

In recent decades, many universities have tried to hold costs down by hiring adjuncts rather than full-time professors. In the early 1970s, adjuncts were about 22 percent of all faculty members nationwide. By 1998, adjuncts were 43 percent. At NYU, the number of part-time faculty members is nearly as large as full-time faculty.

For universities, the advantage of hiring adjuncts is clear: They are paid relatively little and can be hired or dismissed at will. Full-time professors often start at salaries of about $40,000 a year, and they may be eligible for tenure.

Adjuncts are temporary workers in the true sense of the word. They may be paid as little as $1,000 or $2,000 a course and typically receive no health coverage, no pension benefits, and no job guarantee. However, they do not face the same demands to publish, to advise students, or to serve on committees as their full-time coworkers.

Some labor experts say that while it is too early to say what NYU adjuncts might win if they organize, they are likely to win something. Most likely, a win would open the window for more benefits for adjuncts around the nation, for increased salary, pay for office hours, office space, access to technology, and some health care benefits.

At many universities, the biggest concentration of adjuncts is in the continuing education program. And as noted earlier, the demand for continuing education will be more widespread in coming years.

NYU estimates that about a fifth of the adjuncts make their living primarily as adjuncts, piecing together jobs at NYU and other universities. That 20 percent reflects the hard reality in the educational world that there are more people aspiring to tenure-track positions than there are tenure-track positions; no adjunct contract is going to change that.

There is a lot of energy and pro-union sentiment on college campuses and this is part of a much broader wave of organizing everyone from dorm counselors to graduate students.

The campaign at NYU took root as the UAW conducted a successful campaign to organize the NYU graduate assistants. The union had been organizing at universities for more than two decades and represents workers at the University of Massachusetts and Columbia University as well as at NYU.

The AFT expressed a strong interest in representing the NYU adjuncts, arguing that it already represents NYU clerical workers, as well as about 50,000 other adjuncts nationally. "These are educational workers, and this is our area of professional expertise," said Sandra Feldman, AFT president.

The result? The adjuncts at NYU voted to have the United Auto Workers represent them.

IMPLICATIONS

Taken together, these trends represent the forces of truly transformational change in the workplace. It is already destined to alter the day-to-day content of most jobs, as well as the traditional patterns of lifetime employment.

Such changes pose powerful consequences for every individual who enters the workplace, and for the institutional processes—from kindergarten to the college campus—by which our society prepares people for the workplace. This is the K–12 challenge.

Implications for Individuals

To succeed in the new workplace, workers need to have the skills and abilities to add value quickly. This workplace will only reward those "specialized generalists" who have a solid basic education plus deep professional or technical skills. The solid basic education defined in the SCANS competencies appears to fall short of this need.[8]

Everyone will have to be able to do something that adds value *now*—
or be able to learn such value-adding skills quickly—to be considered
for employment in all but the most marginal twenty-first-century jobs.
The liberal arts graduate can increasingly be described as a "literate, unskilled recruit."

While the largest employers such as GM, Lockheed Martin, or the
armed services will have the resources to provide employees with career
counseling and retirement planning, most American workers can expect
to be left to their own devices to manage their own careers. This factor
alone is sufficient to bring classroom-to-career programs into greater
importance from the outset in order to help mold the individual's responsibility. All workers will eventually need an "agent"—much as writ-
ers, actors, and sports figures have agents.

Because many Americans will most likely not have full-time permanent jobs—and even those who do will have no real job security—most
workers will be financially insecure. It means Americans will be forced
to build and maintain liquid savings equivalent to a year or more of income as a shield against periods of unemployment or underemploy-
ment. Today's idea of retirement can be expected to all but disappear
because most Americans will have to work through their sixties, just as
many did fifty years ago.

Implications for the School

Lifelong learning becomes the norm. Educational institutions are
swamped with recurring demand. The new students—especially adults
in midcareer transitions—expect to receive value, quality, speed of delivery, and effectiveness in addition to availability and convenience. Today's K–12 student is tomorrow's continuous education customer.

Education is the critical personal investment for which the consumer
will demand an exceptionally high return. The sheer scale of demand for
differing forms of adult and continuing education, plus the schooling of
the baby boom echo, will overwhelm traditional instructional systems
and methods. It will require technology to play a greater role in the delivery of education. As the schools assimilate new technology, the delivery of education at all levels can be expected to become less labor intensive and more capital intensive. The majority of education resources

can then no longer be devoted to salaries but instead to software, computers, multimedia equipment, and so on.

The trend toward hiring part-time and temporary faculty will continue to pick up speed, mirroring developments in government and industry. The adjunct professor, and many more represented by the autoworkers, can be expected to become the norm on college campuses. Already, fully 38 percent of faculty members work part time; half will be part-timers within five years or less.

Distance learning will further free educational institutions from their geographical boundaries. It will also free educators from educational institutions. The most highly skilled teachers will sell their courses to national and international education packagers and virtual universities. Rather than seeking the security of tenure, these skilled instructors will become "knowledge entrepreneurs," selling their knowledge to a global mass market.

The explosion in education information entrepreneurship will afford students unprecedented access to a limitless variety of courses. Eventually, almost every course taught anywhere in the world will be available to anyone who has access to inexpensive hardware and software. Students will be able to construct their own unique curriculum with courses taught by internationally recognized experts in each field.

This means the teachers of some subjects will become an endangered species. Currently, tens of thousands of teachers provide basic instruction in core subjects such as introductory language, history, biology, math, and so on. New multimedia educational technology will make it possible for a few hundred of the most skilled teachers to provide the instruction of several thousand.

Sound far-fetched? We need to keep in mind that the performance of teachers in larger classroom settings came about from a budgetary necessity. And money isn't expected to flow more freely anytime soon or, owing to higher national priorities, in the foreseeable future.

The Greatest Implication of All

With every passing month, the economic indicators make clear that the United States has recently passed through a historic point in the information revolution. The primary focus of corporate America is no longer the dismantling of our old industrial institutions but rather the creation and staffing of high-value-adding information operations.

Major employers currently create new jobs each year as fast as they are eliminating old jobs, and 60 percent of all those new jobs are offering above-average wages. These are the jobs for which our K–12 classroom teachers need to prepare their students. This is where classroom-to-career initiatives start.

Taken together, the ongoing changes in both the nature of work and the structure of employment foreshadow a seismic quake, a quantum shift in our very understanding of what it means to work, learn, and live.

LEADERSHIP AND VISION

In school, as in life, good intentions are often lost. What we do, not what we say, defines who we are. To align good intentions with effective practice, school leaders need to define a vision, spell out values, and infuse both into every aspect of the daily practices.

Most school leaders love to make strategy, but vision and values are what spawn strategic actions. A strategy without vision dooms any strategy, especially a strategy for change. A true vision shapes hiring, assessment, and promotion of teachers and staff employees, and behavior toward students, parents, and stakeholders.

Vision is a more powerful tool for leading a school organization than any analysis or budget spreadsheet but defining the vision (what the school wants to be) and articulating its values (the principles governing how the school operates) are neither easy nor painless.

The first step in visioning is to assess your school organization, your school district, and your role in the community. What do you do uncommonly well, and how do you fit into the changing landscape? The next step is to take the school management team to an offsite location to look in depth at these questions.

In addition, every new employee in the school needs to go through an extensive visions and values process within ninety days of coming on board and to understand where you are as a school organization. One of the values is having integrity in every school transaction. That's not an earthshaking aspiration, but it needs to have some bite. How we deal with each other is another value. Honesty is the order of the day, in everything from how we start the school day to how we deal with parents. It's all-encompassing and uncompromising.

Matching Effort to Results

Many people in the school may wonder why it is necessary to invest time and effort transmitting your vision and values. If parents keep sending us the same kinds of school kids, why are vision and values a priority? Why not invest in school delivery systems?

Leaders are always tempted to focus on "core" deliverables rather than vision and values but school leaders have to pay attention to both. We invest resources in vision and values because school culture (the way we do things around here) is inseparable from strategy (the way we'll reach the goals we set)—and because we don't want to wake up one day and have a successful school organization that does not have a soul. Without an identity that we purposefully shape, we have no future.

A disciplined approach to vision and values helps teachers and staff understand what's important in the school. It tells us not just what but also how and why we are expected to deliver certain results. To do so calls for assessing people according to two criteria: their current performance and their values. It is not enough to be a cheerleader for values; school leaders have to make tough operating decisions every day.

Leading for Change

Leadership is about managing the constant of change. The world shaping your school is never going to stand still, especially in the new global economy. One technical breakthrough could render your strategy irrelevant overnight. Leaders have no choice but to be fluid, to learn to deal with the ambiguity, to be able to change their operating model. That is why it is so important to have an overarching vision and values to steer by.

Start with the answers. The leader does not have all the answers. No one does. When a team is floundering, we need somebody to step up and say, "I've got an answer." It doesn't even have to be the right answer. If we bring everybody into the process, we may discover quickly that it's not the right answer. It is important to spark action, debate, and a sense of urgency.

Set bold goals.   A bold goal gets everyone's attention, and provides a simple measure of success for everyone in the school. It is not about setting goals so high that teachers simply give their best or burn out trying. Most school systems can quickly realize 20 percent or even 40 percent gains in efficiency once the problem has been properly targeted.

Supply resources.   One of the things leaders provide that others cannot is a commitment of the school organization's time, money, people, or training. The leader's job is to allocate resources, and to do that effectively the leader needs to listen, recognize, and celebrate success.

Coach the team.   When a team clicks, it becomes far more than the sum of its parts; the opposite is also true. Great coaches and effective leaders understand everybody's strength and everybody's weakness. They know how to play to those strengths. The job of the leader is to lift the game of the others on the team. Leaders are accountable for that.[9]

Know education and how to make a difference.   Educators often fail to understand the business they're in or the value they offer. An education leader needs to be sure that everybody understands how you get cost-effective results. You have to break down the results so that people throughout the school enterprise understand how they contribute. People have to be able to go home every day and know that they made a difference.

Understand the human connection.   Always keep in mind the people who are affected by your decisions, and who in turn affect your ability to implement decisions. Leaders cannot be sentimental in shaping the right strategy for the future. Nor can they bully, badger, or fail to respect people. Change efforts succeed when leaders show concern for others. There is a caring way to deal with people even when delivering tough news.

Never compromise on performance.   In the local school, at least until recently, no one's job was ever at risk. If there was a problem employee, that employee was moved to another department. This was demoralizing for the high performers, degrading to the poor performers, and toxic to any change effort. Most poor performers know they're poor performers. With honesty in assessments and fair treatment, most underperformers can accept the fact that they have not made the grade.

Warning Signs

There are many warning signs that can undermine change but several stand out.

One is underestimating the intractable nature of the way things are done "around here." We all have an image of bureaucracy in the school system but bureaucracy is a mind-set. Many of the symptoms of a 30,000-member organization are demonstrated in the 100-member school building. Every organization has a culture—sometimes two or three having a tug-of-war for control. The culture determines how people work together and how they respond to change. No leader can succeed without understanding and shaping the norms at work.

Declaring victory too soon is another. Most of the time when we start change initiatives, we get an immediate lift. The easy pickings are always the first to harvest. It's important to show early results and to celebrate success. However, if we don't work for systematic, continuous improvement, the organization snaps back to its original shape like a large rubber band. True victory is a compelling vision—but it is never really achieved.

Letting people catch their breath is a third. As we reach certain milestones, we tend to want to ease off on the pressure—to slow down, to let people rest. But we cannot! Change has to be part of everyone's job description. We cannot keep people in perpetual firefighting mode, but initially people do have to respond as if their house were on fire. We then need to create a structure and ongoing processes to make change a part of the school.

Fourth, we cannot delegate key elements of the change process. The senior administrator is the leader and he or she has to walk the halls, make the calls, be physically and emotionally present. We cannot tell subordinates to present a plan to the staff and give us a weekly update (a popular approach in Silicon Valley). People love to give PowerPoint presentations, but they hate to actually give us tangible information. The change process starts with how we run our meetings, manage our personal calendar, and share information.

Success is very seductive. Every leader receives glowing reports from the field. We need to discount the good news and pay attention to our doubts. Personal and organizational success is fragile and fleeting. We should take pride in our team's accomplishments, but we need to let people know that the best is always ahead of them.

THE GLOBAL ECONOMY

Years before globalism became a buzzword, business analyst Joel Kotkin was writing about trade and immigration as forces for economic and social vitality. His premise: that dispersed ethnic or national groups who share a strong sense of common identity, a culture of mutual self-help, and a desire to use knowledge for group and personal advancement have powerfully influenced today's global economy.[10] Among the "tribes" he has studied are the Jews, Chinese, Japanese, Indians, and British.[11]

In a world that is both shrinking and splintering, these groups have shown how communities can thrive by looking outward while drawing on inner strengths. First, he stresses, we have to understand history and then use it as a way of looking at the future.

We need to have grounding in history to make the right strategic decisions. The difference today is, it is important to understand history beyond the very narrow view that we were taught as kids—the sort of Anglo-American take on history.

It's important to know that history, but we also have to know about China and Japan and the developing countries because in the future the output of most organizations—particularly the school organization—is tied to those countries. We only need to look around our classrooms and workplaces today to demonstrate this point.

To flourish in the twenty-first century, America is going to have to be a very adept trading country—much like the Dutch or the Italians have been in the past. And that means learning a lot more skills.[12]

NOTES

1. Lawrence Bossidy and Ram Charan, *Execution: The Discipline of Getting Things Done* (New York: Crown Publishing, 2002).

2. Peter F. Drucker, "An Interview with Peter Drucker," *Leader to Leader* (no. 1., Summer 1996).

3. Drucker, "An Interview."

4. Drucker, "An Interview."

5. D. Bell, *The Coming of Post-Industrial Society: A Venture in Social Forecasting* (New York: Basic Books, 1973).

6. Bell, *The Coming of Post-Industrial Society*; Alvin Toffler, *The Third Wave* (New York: Morrow, 1980); J. Naisbitt, *MegaTrends: Ten New Directions Transforming Our Lives* (New York: Warner Books, 1982).

7. Karen W. Arenson, "Two Unions Vie to Represent NYU Adjuncts," *New York Times* (May 27, 2002).

8. "The Secretary's Commission on Achieving Necessary Skills." *What Work Requires of Schools: A SCANS Report for America 2000*. Washington, D.C.: U.S. Department of Labor, 1993.

9. Allen Salowe and Leon Lessinger, *Game Time: The Educator's Playbook for the New Global Economy.* (Lancaster, Penn.: Technomic Publishing, 1997).

10. "The Global Power of Tribes: An Interview with Joel Kotkin," *Leader to Leader* (no. 2, Fall 1996).

11. Joel Kotkin, *Tribes: How Race Religion and Identity Determine Success in the New Global Economy* (New York: Random House, 1993).

12. Peter F. Drucker, *Leader to Leader* (no. 16, Spring 2000).

11

THE DIVERSE WORKFORCE

We need to improve the preparation for the job market our schools do, but even better schools are unlikely to be able to provide adequate skills to support a lifetime of work. Indeed, the need to ensure that our labor force has the ongoing education and training necessary to compete in an increasingly sophisticated world economy is a critical task for the years ahead.[1]

—Alan Greenspan, 1996

What's needed are strong connections to local employers and other local community resources, for valuable and appropriate adult connections, effective career exploration, and school learning standards that align with the standards expected in high-performing global workplaces.

We have the potential for great understanding of the world's people. As our economy is drawn into greater international play, it gives us a bridge to other cultures. If we have people who, through friendship or kinship or cultural ties, can relate to a transnational network or ethnic group, this can open even more doors for us.

THE NEW MELTING POT

It's not always the case that such understandings reveal common interests; sometimes they uncover deep divides that can serve as a red flag. For instance, American companies entered into relationships with Japanese companies with the assumption that Japan looked at transactions in the same way as American and European business partners look at them. That turned out to be a tremendous mistake.

American businesspersons, driven by short-term earnings reports and the daily gyrations of the financial markets, have never understood that the Japanese businessman accepts a lower profit margin for a long period of time in order to gain control of a critical technology in a five-, ten-, or fifteen-year horizon. American company executives and their Euro counterparts do not generally look at the world that way. The executive greed that came out of the debacles of Enron, WorldCom, Adelphia, and Global Crossing, and who knows how many others, is a discouraging example of the still-growing pressures to "push the numbers higher" and have managers and executives personally profit (or survive) from short-term results, whether bogus or otherwise.

As an example, I sat at a meeting-luncheon table one day with two physicians from Iran and remarked that we are all tribal societies. They quickly agreed and this kicked off a three-hour spirited discussion on common grounds. The world as America sees it is not the same world as seen from other continents.

Global tribes offer us another way of viewing the world—a way that has more long-term usefulness than one's organizational culture, which has turned out to be one of the more worthless fads in modern business history. IBM corporate culture did not prove able to withstand the changes that took place in its industry. Ethnic cultures are much more resilient as demonstrated by their existence for centuries and, in some cases, millennia.

We have to understand where *people* are coming from in order to grasp where *things* are coming from. A rational understanding of history, either through reading, attending seminars, by studying the evolution of our economy, or by any other effective method, is infinitely more helpful in dealing with the issue of a more diverse world than imposing the deconstructionist universe of trainers. This is the reason that this book opened with a review of where American education has been and where it is coming from—in a historical context, in an economic context, and in a philosophical context.

Building Bridges to Common Values within Community

Education needs to refocus on the student. There are lots of reasons to gain an understanding of women or African Americans as students, and there are increasing reasons to gain an understanding of immigrant populations. That's where we'll find the most significant differences— among Latinos and Asians, in particular, who come to America with more diverse viewpoints and thus infinitely more prepared to build a bridge to the key social and economic issues of this century.

At the same time, American society is experiencing a severe implosion—the family, the neighborhood, and the community are all breaking down and need to be restrengthened. This cannot be done on a national level; it can only be done locally.

We reviewed the most influential periods in our recent history when—because of the Great Depression, World War II, and the Cold War—we perceived the need for a very strong national state and a very strong national identity.

It's interesting to watch the films of the 1940s and 1950s to grasp the tremendous sense of pride there was in being an American. In many ways, that may have been an artifact of an era in which 95 percent of jobs and teacher exchange took place with other Americans. Now, what do we do when 50 percent of our teaching is conducted with people from other countries?

It's a very different environment from the one we had, but as long as people are working together, living near each other, going to school with each other, and intermarry and socialize with each other, then there's lots of reasons and opportunities for American society to adjust.

Demographics Increasingly Causes a Nervous Reaction

As our population melds into a more diverse bouillabaisse, we also have people fleeing from diversity, looking to re-create an Ozzie-and-Harriet (the American mom and dad of 1950s TV) world that has all but vanished. This is especially common where people are increasingly thrown into an incredibly complex, confusing world. There are people who get nervous or upset when they walk a few blocks down the street and hear four or five different languages, or they are bothered when they see signs in Spanish, Chinese, or Korean. There are many people who do not like it, who do not feel comfortable; perhaps at the root of their discomfort is the fear that they lack the skills to compete.

Many American working-class people, both white and black, feel threatened by immigrants because they fear they cannot compete with these newcomers, cannot work as hard, and are not as determined. This is becoming one of the great dividing lines in American society. For political liberals, there is Montana; for the right-wing types, Idaho; for the "yuppie" types, there are Santa Fe and Taos; for the PC types, there are Boulder and Telluride; for the more elite, Jackson Hole. The effect of all these largely homogeneous communities is to maintain a kind of cultural apartheid, and this can become a source of great future conflict.

MANAGING KNOWLEDGE MEANS MANAGING ONESELF

When the history of our time is written in the twenty-second century, it is likely that the most important event that historians will look back on is not technology, not the Internet, and not e-commerce. It is an unprecedented change in the human condition. For the first time in human history, substantial and rapidly growing numbers of people have choices. For the first time, they will have to manage themselves. And society is totally unprepared for it.[2]

Throughout history, practically nobody had choices; even in the most highly developed countries, the overwhelming majority followed their fathers' lines of work—if they were lucky. If your father was a peasant farmer, you were a peasant farmer. If he was a craftsman, you were a craftsman. There was only downward mobility; there was no upward mobility.

I still see in my mind's eye my own parents battling over this issue. Both were first-generation Americans emigrating from Ukraine to escape the czar and the pogroms. Each saw the New World through different eyes. My brother, a Phi Beta Kappa scholar, wanted to go on to become a CPA. Mom supported him in this goal. Dad wanted him to follow in his footsteps and go into the family dry cleaning business. Dad accused Mom of wanting her children to move up the social ladder. Mom insisted that she did not want to see her children struggle as hard as did their father and therefore she saw education as the stepping-stone to a better life. Mom insisted that all her children should have the choices she never had. My mother never learned to read or write but understood sociology and human behavior. Well, my brother got his MBA, became a CPA, and later directed the Education Division for the American Institute of Certified Public Accountants—and no one was more proud of him than my father.

Today, American education has given a large number of people many more choices. What is more, they will have more than one career, because the working life span of a person is fast approaching sixty years—three times what it was in 1900.

ABUNDANCE OF CHOICES

Knowledge gives us choice. It explains why we now have female firefighters and police officers in the same jobs as men. Historically, men and women had always had equal participation in the labor force—the idea of the idle housewife is a nineteenth-century delusion. Men and women simply did different jobs.

Knowledge work knows no gender because men and women do the same jobs. This, too, is a major change in the human condition. To succeed in this new world, we first need to learn who we are.

Few people can define what they are good at and even fewer ask themselves the question. In contrast, many are proud or even brag about their ignorance. There are managers who are proud of the fact that they cannot read a balance sheet and boast about it. In the new post–WorldCom and Enron environment, corporate accountability and the threat of jail time are going to change this. Other managers who are prideful of a lack of computer skills will find it increasingly risky to not keep up with the data and information. If an executive wants to be effective today, he or she needs to be able to read and understand a financial statement and operate a computer.

There are accountants who are equally proud of the fact that they cannot get along with people! They are proud of being "numbers savvy" in a people world. That, of course, is nothing to be proud of, because anyone can *learn* to work smoothly with others. And in the complex business world of creative corporate finance and judgment-driven accounting practices, these professionals had better understand what someone else is up to or risk serious repercussions. It is not hard, after all, to learn manners—and manners are what allow people to get along.

In an information-rich global economy, all of us need to *learn* who we are, which is the first step to *knowing* who we are. It's not very difficult. The key to it—what Leonardo da Vinci and Mozart did—is to record the results of our decisions. Every time you do something that is important, write down what you expect will happen.

It's easy to understand our strengths by tracking our results. Still, most of us underestimate our own strengths. We take them for granted. What we are good at comes easy, and we believe that unless it comes hard, it can't be very good. As a result, we don't know our strengths, and we don't know how we can build on them.

Understanding our strengths, articulating our values, knowing where we belong—these are also essential to addressing one of the great challenges of organizations: improving the abysmally low productivity of knowledge workers. By productivity we are using the classical economic definition of performing professional work both efficiently and effectively. The productivity of the schoolteacher, for instance, has not improved, and may have shrunk in the past seventy years. Schoolteachers, for many reasons (some not of their own making) have become significantly less effective and certainly operate with less and less efficiency. Of course, teachers in the 1920s will tell us they enjoyed the advantage of not having to attend faculty meetings.

Effective organizations put people in jobs in which they can do the most good. They place people—and allow people to place themselves—according to their strengths. The historic shift to self-management offers organizations ways to develop and motivate knowledge workers.

The greatest competitive advantage of the United States is that we attract top knowledge workers from around the world—not because they can earn more money over here but because they are treated as colleagues, not as subordinates. Knowledge workers do not believe they are paid to work 9 A.M. to 5 P.M.; they believe they're paid to be effective. Organizations that understand this, strip away everything that gets in the knowledge workers' way, and are able to attract, hold, and motivate the best performers. This is the single biggest factor for American competitive advantage in the next twenty-five years.

These factors are also the greatest challenge to American students who mistakenly come to believe they are entitled to the best jobs at the best pay just because they are American.

HIGH-PERFORMING SCHOOLS ALIGN
ACTION AND VALUES

School administrators spend too much time drafting and redrafting vision statements, mission statements, values statements, purpose statements, aspiration statements, and so on. They spend nowhere near enough time trying to align their school organization with the values and visions already in place.

Vision is one of the least understood and most overused terms in the English language. Vision is simply a combination of three basic elements: (1) the organization's fundamental reason for existence (often called mission or purpose), (2) the timeless unchanging core values (what we are here to do and do well), and (3) the achievable aspirations for its own future (what we want to become when we grow up). Of these, the most important to a great enduring organization is *core values*.

It's all well and good to understand the vision concept but there is a big difference between being a school organization with a vision statement and one that evolves into a visionary organization. The difference lies in creating alignment to preserve core values, to reinforce purposes, and to stimulate ongoing progress towards its aims. When a school leader has superb alignment, a visitor could drop into the school from another planet and infer the vision without having to read it on paper.[3]

Creating alignment is a two-part process. The first is to identify and correct the misalignments. The second is creating new alignments, or what we call "systems with teeth."

Identifying misalignment starts with looking around the organization, talking to people, getting input, and asking, "If these are our core values and this is fundamentally why we exist, what obstacles are getting in our way?"

Most school organizations claim they respect and trust their teachers and staff to do the right thing. Then, they undermine that statement by doing X, Y, and Z. These contradictions come from the everyday experience of teachers. In one case, the administration might encourage more "creative" approaches to classroom management, then issues written edicts, too often followed by subtle or sharp rebukes for how a particular matter is handled. And there is the building principal whose school policies flap in the wind each time there is a board of education meeting. Or the front office that quietly monitors teacher hours as means of gaining productivity, though not yielding any greater efficiency. Such actions are counterintuitive and most often serve to deflate the remaining enthusiasm a teacher might have for facing the day.

The misalignments exist not because the statements are false; these schools believe what they say. The misalignments occur because years of ad hoc policies and practices become institutionalized and obscure the school's underlying values. The way we do things around here becomes a built-in bad habit.

For example, how often have we witnessed a school launch a new program or service without coordinating its internal processes, and as a result create problems for stakeholders? To make sure this doesn't repeat itself endlessly, school leaders need to avoid sign-off procedures for each new service that remains embedded in school operations long after people have forgotten why it was created.

As for organizational values, we cannot set them; we can only discover them. Nor can we instill new core values into people. Core values are not something people buy into. People need to be predisposed to holding them as values.

Leaders often ask, "How do we get people to share our core values?" We don't. Rather, the task is to *find* people who are already prone to sharing the core values. We need to attract and then retain these people and let those who are less inclined to sharing the school's core values go elsewhere.

Core values are timeless. These do not change. Practices and strategies should be changing all the time. Cultural norms should never stop changing. A timeless school core value is freedom of intellectual inquiry. A practice to support that core value is academic tenure. However, there is now evidence to suggest that the practice of tenure probably needs to be changed or discarded because it no longer serves the purposes for which it was intended and originally created. But if we suggest that school districts should seriously think about changing the tenure system, the average teacher or administrator is likely to say, "Never! You're violating our core values."

That protest comes about from a failure to distinguish between values and practices. The core value is freedom of inquiry; tenure is a practice.

Frequently, institutions cling doggedly to practices that are, in truth, nothing more than familiar habits that fit comfortably like an old pair of shoes. As a result, educators fail to change the things that need to change. And defending outmoded education practices under the banner of core values might actually betray the educator's true core values.

LEADING TRANSITION: A NEW MODEL FOR CHANGE

Change is nothing new to leaders or their constituents. The local school cannot be endlessly managed by following yesterday's practices to achieve tomorrow's success. Conditions change and yesterday's assumptions and practices no longer work. There must be innovation, and innovation means change. Schools must meet the needs of their time.

Books, seminars, and consultants claim to help schools "manage change" but fall short. Such tools neglect the dynamics of personal and school transition that help determine the outcome of any change effort. As a result, they fail to address the leader's need to coach others through the transition process. And they fail to acknowledge the fact that leaders themselves usually need coaching before they can effectively coach others.[4]

In years past, leaders simply ordered changes. Even today, many view it as a straightforward process: establish a taskforce; lay out what needs to be done, when, and by whom. Then all that seems left for the organization is (an innocent-sounding phrase!) *to implement the plan*. Many leaders imagine that to make change work, people need to follow the plan's implicit map, which shows how to get from here (where things stand now) to there (where they'll stand after the plan is *implemented*).

"There" is also where the organization needs to be if it is to survive, so anyone who has looked at the situation with a reasonably open mind can see that the change isn't optional. It's essential.

Why don't people "just do it"? And what is the leader to do when *they* just don't do it, when people do not make needed changes, when deadlines are missed, when costs run over budget, and valuable workers get so frustrated they look to jump ship?

Leaders who try analyzing this question after the fact are likely to review the effort and its implementation, but details of the intended change are not the issue. Whatever it was, the change that once seemed so obviously necessary languishes like last week's flowers.

Transition occurs in the course of every attempt at change. Transition is the state that change puts people into. The *change* is external (the different policy, practice, or structure that the leader is trying to bring about) while *transition* is internal (a psychological reorientation that people have to go through before the change can work).

The trouble is, most leaders imagine that transition is automatic, that it occurs simply because change is happening—but it doesn't. Just because the computers are on everyone's desk doesn't mean that the new individually accessed data warehouse is used to transform operations the way the consultants promised it would.[5]

Even when change shows signs of working, there is the issue of timing, for transition happens much more slowly than change. That is why the ambitious timetable that the leader lays out to the school board often turns out to have been wildly optimistic: It was based on fully accomplishing the *change*, not on getting the people through the process of *transition*.

Transition takes longer because it requires that people undergo a process that tends to be upsetting. People have to let go of the way things used to be—and, worse yet, the way that they themselves used to be. Folk wisdom tells us, "You can't steal second base with your foot still on first." You have to leave where you are, and many people have spent their entire lives standing on first base. It isn't just a personal preferences we are asking someone to give up. We are asking them to let go of the old way of engaging in tasks that made them successful in the past. We ask them to let go of what feels to them like their whole world of experience, their sense of identity, even reality itself.

TAKING THE LONG VIEW

English economist John Maynard Keynes is remembered for saying, "In the long-run, we're all dead" and the phrase has repeatedly been used as justification for avoiding long-haul planning. Today, with the speed of communications and change, our lives can almost be measured in "dog years" where seemingly seven years of stress and change are packed into one year of living.

Today's classroom-to-career movement is caught in a paradox where targeted funding is quickly on the wane. The core ideas and principles of classroom-to-career programs are powerful and they are popping up in many different places and ways.

There is a push toward smaller, more personalized learning communities in large comprehensive high schools. These often take a career focus.

Classroom–community partnerships continue to grow and deepen, though some of the newest and best may see themselves as part of efforts to raise academic achievement, strengthen after-school programming, or improve regional economic development because employers need better-skilled employees.

Many small, innovative public and private charter high schools are creating curricula and community-based learning experiences that correspond with classroom-to-career principles.

Service-learning initiatives and community-based youth arts programs, while frequently divorced from the classroom-to-career movement, share many of the basic design principles and program components.

Here's the contradiction: If we only take the short view, there is cause for concern about the future of classroom-to-career initiatives. However, if we take the long view, the picture is quite different. It is our view that the nation is currently in the midst of a dynamic era. The twentieth-century-factory model of schooling, and particularly high school education, is as much a dinosaur as the factory model of industrial production it mimics.

Ted Sizer, chairman of Essential Schools, has repeatedly said schools are no longer the repository of knowledge, as they were in the Middle Ages or even at the turn of the twentieth century. Knowledge is everywhere; if anything, it is too easily accessible. Schools need to become the place where the skills of analysis, discernment, synthesis, and *use* of knowledge are taught and learned.

Technology, organization, a more networked economy, growth of entrepreneurship, and other such changes will ultimately drive changes in our system of educating and preparing people for productive careers and rewarding lives. Education reformers need to ask: How quickly will such changes occur, what institutional form will they take, and what strategies can be pursued to speed them up?

Given current trends, classroom-to-career elements are likely to be more commonplace and less controversial in the economy and learning systems of this next generation. We're likely to see:

- An academically rigorous approach that is active, experiential, and contextual and that focuses on skills for solving problems in real situations;
- Strong connections to local employers for valuable adult connections, effective career exploration, and school learning standards that align with standards expected in high-performing global workplaces;
- Better strategies for helping young people make postsecondary choices, combine school and work, and earn postsecondary credits, credentials, and skills; and
- A more personalized, less standardized education that enables individuals to discover and develop something that they are good at.

What remains controversial are not these elements but how we get from here to there to change the local school, update the learning and instructional standards, help prepare the routes to career success, and increase the students' daily experiences as they prepare for a future toward these ends. And how do we ensure that positive outcomes are not unequally distributed because of social class, race, or other accident of birth?

More and more, we stress removing the local school from its isolation and this is one of the more important contributions employers can make. Employers want to know what potential employees know and what they can do. There is clear evidence that employers look for specific indicators of a job applicant's abilities; frustration with the high school transcript and college diploma runs deep. To remedy such shortcomings, employer groups (particularly those in the demanding knowledge fields) have moved ahead to create industry-based standards and certifications that have real meaning in the job market.

Demographics will keep employers coming back. As long as the U.S. economy stays healthy, the combination of large numbers of soon-to-retire older workers with a relatively small cohort of young people means that employers will be more willing to try newer, less conventional ways to identify potential employees. This includes novel partnerships with schools and colleges. The rapid expansion of collaborative projects such as Automotive Youth Educational Systems (AYES), established first by General Motors and now run as an industry consortium, demonstrate the potential.[6]

But good old political realities can never be completely ignored. The opportunities are significant, emerging research is promising, and local progress around the country is impressive. However, these developments are not powerful enough in the short run to reverse the political isolation of classroom-to-career programs among policymakers in many states.

We need to focus relentlessly on data and outcomes.[7] Are local classroom-to-career efforts improving young peoples' future choices and success? That is the key question. Classroom-to-career programs need to demonstrate their effect on traditional academic outcomes (i.e., grades and standardized test scores).

We need to support leading innovators and target additional resources to help support programs and initiatives that demonstrate promise and progress in achieving quality outcomes for participating young people.

We need to strengthen partnerships and intermediaries. One of the most important outcomes of classroom-to-career initiatives to date has been the strengthening of both local business-to-school partnerships *and* local intermediary organizations that convene and connect schools, businesses, and other community resources.

We need to reach out to new allies. In today's political environment, many potentially valuable and powerful new alliances are available to classroom-to-career advocates. An important one is postsecondary institutions. As key customers of CTC programs, these can help influence program standards. And they are themselves searching for ways to improve quality for a largely working population of students.

We believe these proposed short- and long-term strategies can help advance the classroom-to-career agenda. It can help promote quality and improvement, sustain state and community efforts already taking root and showing results, and support the classroom-to-career community.

SCHOOLS CANNOT BE ALL THINGS TO
ALL PEOPLE AND SUCCEED

Whenever an institution goes beyond a narrow focus, it ceases to perform. Many hospitals that tried to go beyond sickness care into "health education" and "illness prevention" have been miserable failures.

There are many reasons why the local public school is in trouble. Surely the one reason that stands out is that we have, of necessity, tried to make the local school the agent of social reform and social integration. Schools in all other countries, including countries that have serious social and population problems of their own (for example, France, with its immigrant population of over two million Muslims) have stuck to the single goal of teaching children to read. And they are generally successful in this single endeavor.

A striking social phenomenon of the last thirty years in the United States is the explosive growth of the new "megachurches" (now being emulated in Europe) that rest on the institution's dedication to a single purpose: the spiritual development of the parishioners. The decline of their predecessors, the liberal Protestant churches of the early years of the twentieth century, can largely be traced to their trying to accomplish too many things at the same time—above all, in their trying to be organs of social reform as well as spiritual leaders.

"The strength of the modern pluralist organization," writes Drucker, "is that it is a single-purpose institution. And that strength has to be maintained. But at the same time the community has to be maintained—and in many cases it has to be rebuilt."[8]

So we come full circle to how we balance the common good and the special purpose of the local school for an increasingly diverse population. If we are unable to achieve this integration, the local school will surely destroy itself because it will erode—and with its decline, help to destroy the local community. But if at the same time institutions abandon their single purpose or even allow that purpose to be weakened, the local school will destroy itself through lack of performance.

This leads us around to need for a different mind-set. There is need for the acceptance of leaders in every single institution and in every single sector that they, as leaders, have two responsibilities.

They are responsible and accountable for the performance of their institutions—the local school—and that requires them and their institutions to be concentrated, focused, and limited.

They are also responsible for the community as a whole—and this requires commitment. It requires a willingness to accept that other institutions have different values, respect for these values, and willingness to learn what these values are. It requires hard work. But above all, it requires commitment, conviction, and dedication to the common good.

The local school is autonomous and has to do its own work the way each instrument in an orchestra plays only its own part. But there is also the score, the community. Only if each individual instrument contributes to the score is there music. Otherwise, there is only noise.

NOTES

1. Alan Greenspan, chairman, Federal Reserve Board, Humprehey-Hawkins Testimony (February 20, 1996).

2. See Allen Salowe and Leon Lessinger, *Solutions: Tools and Strategies for Schools* (Lanham, Md.: Scarecrow Education Press, 2002).

3. Salowe and Lessinger, *Solutions*.

4. Salowe and Lessinger, *Solutions*.

5. Peter F. Drucker, *Leader to Leader* (no. 16, Spring 2000).

6. AYES is a "dynamic partnership among participating automotive manufacturers, participating local dealers, and selected local high schools/tech prep schools. Its goal is to encourage bright students with a good mechanical aptitude to pursue careers in the ever-changing fields of automotive service technology or collision repair/refinish, and to prepare them for entry-level positions or challenging academic options." More information about AYES can be found at www.ayes.org.

7. Drucker, *Leader to Leader*.

8. Drucker, *Leader to Leader*.

INDEX

Ackoff, Russell, 145, 146

Black Alliance for Educational
    Options (BAEO) dropout study,
    31–34

car making and teaching, similarities,
    175–177
change:
    align action and values, 193
    Cold War, 52
    easier said than done,
        128–131
    from high tech to high touch,
        120–122
    implications, 177–180
    least resistant to, teachers,
        122–123
    long view to, 197
    management and control of
        classroom, teachers need,
        136–137

need to focus for, 148
new model for, 195
parents, apple falls near the
    tree, 134–135
Plainfield, NJ, 1–2
structural change, puzzle of,
    146
systems, understanding for,
    147–148
teachers, setting the tone for,
    131–134
urban stress, teachers and,
    137–138
warning signs, 183
where we start, 152–155
chronology of change:
    1900–1920, 24
    1921–1936, 25
    1937–1945, 25–26
    1946–1959, 26
    1960–1980, 26–28
    1993–present, 28–29

classroom to career:
    building blocks and initiatives,
        111–116
    business partners, what schools
        need from, 117–120
    career academy, 139–142
    case studies, 96–103
    federal stepchild, 95
    linking to initiatives, 161–166
    National Alliance for Business,
        94
    Philadelphia, PA, 92–94
    programs and the future, 167
    success stories, 105–111
cultural diversity, 23–24

Deming, W. Edwards, 155
Drucker, Peter, 167

Georgia O'Keeffe Elementary
    School, Mrs. Edwards' class,
    116–117, 154, 156

Head to Head, 3

initiatives:
    Canada, 76
    Clarkson College, NY, 72–73
    employer's role, 91–92
    Honda of America, 73
    Maryland and Baldrige, 74
    North Carolina, 75–76
    Ohio Learning First Alliance, 73
    student, 88–89
    Tennessee and Baldrige, 71–72
interdependent action, 3–4

larger community, connecting the
    school to, 5–7
leadership and vision, 180–182

*Meeting the Highly Qualified
    Teachers Challenge*, report of,
    9–11

our time:
    approach to learning, new,
        89–91
    building and classroom
        performance, gap between,
        60–64
    business and learning, linking
        of, 79–82
    classroom to career, linking,
        86–87
    community and school,
        planning for, 64–68
    economic perspective of, 37–40
    educate, minimal obligations of
        government to, 56–59
    global economy, 184
    local school, good practices,
        116–117
    meeting the needs of, 13–20
    missing links of, 78–79
    new melting pot in, 188–190
    new relationships in, 171
    organization in, 170
    parents and schools, linking to,
        82–83
    planning horizon for, 168
    questions for, ix–x
    rearview mirror, view in, 173
    schools, not all things to all
        people in, 200
    teacher's job in, 170
    unavoidable link to, 127–128

quality:
    Baldrige Program for schools,
        157–161

ISO 9000, 156
Total Quality Management
  (TQM), 156

Smith, Adam:
  applied to government, 45–46
  economic view, 40
  laws of the market, 41–45
  motivation, 47
  why explained?, 48–50

strategies, building capacity for, xi

teacher backlash, 76–77
tools that work:
  measures, 124–125
  refrigerator door language,
    125–126
  vision of success, 123–124

Whyte, William, 171

ABOUT THE AUTHOR

Allen E. Salowe is a senior fellow of the Florida Institute of Education (a Type-I State University System Education Improvement Center) and senior fellow of the Florida Center for Electronic Communication (a Type-II Research Center at Florida Atlantic University). He served as president of the Plainfield (N.J.) School Board and as adjunct professor of economics and management. This is his sixth book for improving public education.

He is a former senior vice-president of planning for ITT Community Development Corporation; senior operations executive for ITT World Headquarters, and group planning director, Champion International. He served as economic and financial adviser to Florida Community Development Special Taxing Districts.

Mr. Salowe holds a master's of business administration in management from Nova Southeastern University and a bachelor of arts in economics from the University of Miami and is AICP registered (American Institute of Certified Planners).